David
July '84

SHAKESPEARE'S USE OF DREAM AND VISION

Shakespeare's Use of Dream and Vision

JOHN ARTHOS

Il y a des hommes océans en effet.
VICTOR HUGO

ROWMAN AND LITTLEFIELD
Totowa, New Jersey

First published in the United States 1977
by ROWMAN AND LITTLEFIELD, Totowa, N.J.

Library of Congress Cataloging in Publication Data

Arthos, John, 1908–
   Shakespeare's Use of Dream and Vision

   Includes index.
    1. Shakespeare, William, 1564–1616—Technique.
I. Title.
PR2995.A75   822.3'3   76-40996
ISBN 0-87471-912-7

Printed in Great Britain

Cytherea! thow blysful lady swete,
That madest me this sweven for to mete.

CONTENTS

PREFACE

Dreams, ghosts, apparitions—these are among the greatest delights in Shakespeare, he gives them a multitude of forms and discovers contrivances for their use that are as charming or awesome in spectacle as they are rich in meaning. Mercutio's fancies and Juliet's forebodings, the one all but gratuitous, the other central to the play's movement, reveal how close to the playwright's conceptions at any moment is the sense of realms of being across the threshhold of the waking sight.

We may come to think that Shakespeare thinks of the visionary as inherent in the character of tragedy and comedy, and it is almost second nature for him, it appears, to include the supernatural in the representation of history. In the last plays the apparitions and visions are so splendid and announce their burden with such authority the audience itself must often feel as some in the dramas do, that on waking we shall find it truth. This is what one of the twins as much as said in *A Comedy of Errors* in speaking of a 'glorious supposition'. And since Shakespeare from the beginning made such use of these devices, and they bear such a wealth of interest, we find ourselves inevitably asking if there is some basis in the reasoning and beliefs of the playwright's own that accounts for their charm.

Very often we acknowledge the suggestion of powers we are induced to think of as fate or destiny or providence but we have learned that in plays so richly conceived as these we must never settle for abstractions. We draw many inferences that point even to the systematic elaboration of ideas—*Macbeth* requires us to—

although in the end we rarely feel we may go farther than Professor R. H. West has in calling upon the phrase, 'the outer mystery'. We cannot mistake the seriousness with which Shakespeare exploits the sense of such powers—even in what we know to be Prospero's conjurings the figures of gods point to the consideration of real agencies. Shakespeare dissuades us from referring these to explicit doctrines—of fate or providence, for example—and he as clearly refrains from assuring us there is no direction whatever in what we accept as so much like the world we know. There are many reasons we should rest content with accepting many of these intimations simply as responding to our need to marvel, seeing in such representations that faithfulness to the sense of things the ancients honored in saying that thought begins and ends in wonder. Yet while we impose restraints upon any inclination we have to discover allegories we know that in these works thought is as profoundly engaged as it would be in philosophy, and as recalcitrant to reduction.

From the beginning even the most high-spirited comedies are informed with intellectuality. We notice certain ideas recurring; we may single out some of these as of great importance, in themselves and in contributing to the form of the works; others may receive less emphasis. We can have very little confidence we shall be equal to the comprehensiveness that is Shakespeare's hallmark, yet we are right to believe that we recognize certain central and abiding concerns, some to which Shakespeare returns again and again as to a magnet.

One of these, certainly, is that men live with truth and know it to be truth. Shakespeare from the beginning made of this almost everything he could although soon enough it was obvious it did not fulfil the promises so many in his writings took it to be making. Adonis held to this confidence in repelling Venus—

> Before I know myself, seek not to know me.

Troilus held to it as to a redeeming power—

> I am as true as truth's simplicity,
> And simpler than the infancy of truth.

At the heart of all such protestation is faith in being able to attain some all-satisfying reward in following the injunction, Know thyself. But as for what was finally required, the promise failed as one after another learned how carelessly life could be snuffed out and the purest and most dedicated of humans could be undone. The idea was infinitely alluring. When, through disguises or mistakes, individuals were taken to be other than themselves and they discovered even love could be misplaced, ways were still found to hold to a belief in constancy. Antipholus of Syracuse, Berowne, and Valentine could go wholly wrong and yet somehow remain steadfast, or believe they were. The comedies, at least, seem to warrant their convictions. But with the histories, full of terrible frustrations and catastrophic evil, the aspirations many in the comedies thought would be substantiated came to judgment. The hope of Antipholus, Berowne's appeal to a Promethean fire, Valentine's conviction of transcendent union turn to ashes for the sixth Henry and the second Richard. This of course was but one of the issues the action of the dramas would turn on, but in its nature one that invited the introduction of whatever would challenge the authority of sense. The simplest and clearest of faiths, when questioned, called upon visitations, dreams, even superstitions for support. The trust in recourse to the soul's pure truth was rooted in aspiration as much as in knowledge. The assurance of satisfaction, the possibility of defeat, were defined in the extremes of heavenly rewards and hellish deprivations. Silvia's holiness, Hermia's and Helena's falling out, Hippolyta's 'great constancy', all are witness to the profundity of the issues. We see this as suggestively indicated as anywhere in Bottom's groping for words with which to tell his dream. He himself would appear to be anything but such a person for whom the extremes of satisfaction and denial were of concern, and yet in that stumbling about to find the words for those wonderful moments when he was so loved, confused now—man's hand cannot taste, man's eye hath not heard—he is revealing the sense of a power beyond that pointed to even in Caliban's heavenly music, or in Troilus's faith. Saint Paul had developed the ancient figure of the world's body, for him having become Christ's, and had pursued the thought of how men who were confused might think: 'And if the ear shall say, Because I am not the eye, I am not of the body; is it therefore not of the body? And again: If the whole body were an eye, where was the hearing?' He turned to one way of confusion after another, and Saint John in the First Epistle (as Professor W. M. Merchant has observed) speaks even more directly to the state in which Bottom found himself: 'That which was from the beginning, which we have heard, which we have seen with our eyes, which we have looked upon, and our hands have handled, of the Word of life.'

Again and again in the plays confusion and darkness of spirit are lit up by the light of dreams and visions, sometimes in such limited terms as we become acquainted with in *Love's Labour's Lost*; sometimes as with Bottom in the suggestion of Christian revelation; always complexly, whether in that lovely conceit of glory Antipholus played with—

> in that glorious supposition think
> He gains by death that hath such means to die;

or in Prospero's confidence in the disappearance of the globe.

When we are drawn to consider philosophic and metaphysical matters, relating images and disquisitions to the action of Shakespeare's plays, we are inevitably reminded that once it was common to admire his learning while denying him intellectual power. The wheel has turned, of course. The learning astonishes us as much as ever but now we take for granted that it fed his understanding. We may notice in Castiglione a particular phrase he made use of in *Hamlet* but we go on from there in acknowledging that it is its general Platonic import he is developing. Often we are not able to point to particular texts as sources, and we must believe that much extended reasoning came to him through talk with friends and in the bustle of affairs, from knowing what Chapman was engaged with, or what was being thrashed out in some controversy among Puritans. He would have known what Raleigh and Marston and Bruno were involved in and pursuing with such passion. As for what we find as sources in his reading—if, for example, we believe he was remembering the very words of Saint John's First Epistle—we may be confident he had meditated on them, he would never have been merely worded.

In short, when we look at these writings composed to entertain, pursuing ideas and drawing for illustration upon a wide experience, we are merely supposing that Shakespeare was coming to terms with the interests and affairs of the members of his audience. In one of Hamlet's most famous stage-directions we hear Shakespeare telling us it was his business to be in touch with the spirit of the age. It is with this in mind that I commence this study with a consideration of *The Phœnix and Turtle*, a poem that appeared in a volume to which, in making their own contributions, Jonson, Marston, and Chapman were less discrete than Shakespeare in revealing their debts to specific philosophies. Looking at Shakespeare's poem in this setting makes it plain, I believe, why one should be prepared to consider metaphysical matters elsewhere in his writings.

These studies thereafter center on a handful of plays. Others might have been reviewed, but these few—*A Midsummer Night's Dream*, *Julius Caesar*, *Hamlet*, *The Tempest*—offer more than enough opportunity to explore matters of deepest concern. It may be that in the uses we see him making of the supernatural we notice a certain progression in Shakespeare's thought. For my part I am not confident of this, but there can be no doubt that both theatrically and intrinsically the visionary always attracted him. This study is offered in observing something we may learn from that lasting interest.

A section of the chapter 'The Undiscovered Country' is reprinted through the kind permission of the editors of *Comparative Drama*, where it first appeared.

The Dream and the Vision

I

Let the bird of lowdest lay,
On the sole *Arabian* tree,
Herauld sad and trumpet be:
To whose sound chaste wings obay.

But thou shriking harbinger,
Foule precurrer of the fiend,
Augour of the fevers end,
To this troupe come thou not neere.

From this Session interdict
Every foule of tyrant wing,
Save the Eagle feath'red King,
Keepe the obsequie so strict.

Let the Priest in Surples white,
That defunctive Musicke can,
Be the death-devining Swan,
Lest the *Requiem* lacke his right.

And thou treble dated Crow,
That thy sable gender mak'st,
With the breath thou giv'st and tak'st,
Mongst our mourners shalt thou go.

Here the Antheme doth commence,
Love and Constancie is dead,

15

Phœnix and the *Turtle* fled,
In a mutuall flame from hence.

So they loved as love in twaine,
Had the essence but in one,
Two distincts, Division none,
Number there in love was slaine.

Hearts remote, yet not asunder;
Distance and no space was seene,
Twixt this *Turtle* and his Queene;
But in them it were a wonder.

So betweene them Love did shine,
That the *Turtle* saw his right,
Flaming in the *Phœnix* sight;
Either was the others mine.

Propertie was thus appalled,
That the selfe was not the same:
Single Natures double name,
Neither two nor one was called.

Reason in it selfe confounded,
Saw Division grow together,
To themselves yet either neither,
Simple were so well compounded.

That it cried, how true a twaine,
Seemeth this concordant one,
Love hath Reason, Reason none,
If what parts, can so remaine.

Whereupon it made this *Threne*,
To the *Phœnix* and the *Dove*,
Co-supremes and starres of Love,
As *Chorus* to their Tragique Scene.

THRENOS

Beautie, Truth, and Raritie,
Grace in all simplicitie,
Here enclosde, in cinders lie.

Death is now the *Phœnix* nest,
And the *Turtles* loyall brest,
To eternitie doth rest.

Leaving no posteritie,
Twas not their infirmitie,
It was married Chastitie.

Truth may seeme, but cannot be,
Beautie bragge, but tis not she,
Truth and Beautie buried be.

To this urne let those repaire,
That are either true or faire,
For these dead Birds, sigh a prayer.

The first words of *The Phœnix and Turtle*, announcing a call of birds to a requiem mass, are strange, archaic, and even ominous. But as those who are to come are called by name and others are debarred we learn the ceremony is to be in honor of everything that is excellent, love and beauty and truth—the note of the strange and the forbidding is all but silenced in invoking what most graces humans. A succession of abstract words, virtues as it were embodied, brings into the account of a rite to be performed by birds the suggestion of human presences, and when one such, Reason, at the end is heard chanting, asking for a prayer for the dead, we realize that what has been wild and fantastic in it all is an index to the dread and hope humans know in contemplating the loss of life. Through the strangeness and the fear and then in notes of exultation we come to feel a power in the poem as astonishing as the range and depth of the thought it draws on.

In the art as in the matter we may believe we see what was stirring most profoundly in Shakespeare's mind. C. S. Lewis meant this and more when he remarked that 'here we feel that we have been admitted to the *natura naturans* from which the *natura naturata* of the plays proceeded: as though we had reached the garden of Adonis and seen where Imogens and Cordelias are made.'[1] Others speak of finding the evidence of a 'mystical' experience that made possible the 'vision' of the tragedies and the romances.[2] There is indeed no end to the reflections the poem gives rise to, and most provocatively when we try to discover what we make of it as an expression of conviction.

Shakespeare's poem is one of several in a collection honoring a pair whose love was exemplary. The volume was printed with the title *Loves Martyr*, the name given to the introductory poem by Robert Chester. Chester's poem bore the further title, 'Rosalins Complaint, Metaphorically applied to Dame Nature at a Parliament held (in the high Star-chamber) by the Gods, for the preseruation and increase of Earths beauteous Phoenix.' This was followed by a group of short poems by a number of writers. The legend of the bird regenerated from its ashes provided the initial device of this and some of the other poems in the collection.

Chester's poem tells how Nature, a magnificent being who fears that her most loved creation, the Phoenix, will die, and without issue, ascends into the heavens to plead for her favorite's life. At first the gods were not inclined to listen but when Nature showed them a marvellously beautiful image of the Phoenix and they realized that the original would be even more beautiful, Jove and the other gods granted her request. The Phoenix was escorted to Paphos, there to meet with a Turtle-Dove. The two make a fire of fragrant woods according to their knowledge of a necessary ritual. A pelican and her young are in attendance. Here takes place the fiery death, the 'Sacrifice of bloud', through which the Phoenix will be regenerated. At the moment of death the Phoenix asks for something other than had been in Nature's prayer—

> O holy, sacred and pure perfect fire, . . .
> Accept into your euer hallowed flame,
> Two bodies, from the which may spring one name.

The Turtle was asking for a like consummation—

> Do not deny me *Phœnix* I must be
> A partner in this happy Tragedy.

The poem had commenced with the thought that a perfect being ought not to be allowed to die, but other meanings were included when it came to seem that that perfection had been made still more perfect through love. And the regeneration originally prayed for, which would have been that either of prolonged life or of survival through the birth of offspring, now is conceived as a life like that of the gods, apart from the earth, a metamorphosis in which two beings become one through the instrumentality of sacrifice and death.

The poems following *Loves Martyr* were separated from it under the title, 'Diverse Poeticall Essaies on the former Subiect; viz. the Turtle and Phoenix. Done by the best and chiefest of our moderne writers, with their names subscribed to their particular works.' There is an 'Invocatio' signed by 'Vatum Chorus', in which in the name of the writers whose poems follow a libation is metaphorically offered to 'Apollo & Pierides' in asking for inspiration. The word 'Chorus' is the right one, for not only do the writers keep to the theme of the love of the Phoenix and Turtle, they do so in presenting meanings that suggest they had been talking among themselves about the use poetry could make of philosophy when writing of death and the immortal yearnings love fortifies.

One brief poem, contrary to the words of the title-page, is signed 'Ignoto'. The others are ascribed to Shakespeare, Marston, Chapman, and Jonson.

There are some matters that are not coordinated. The poets do not agree on the sex of the birds. Then, the poem of Marston's that follows Shakespeare's, and that has the appearance of being a response to it, begins by denying, at least rhetorically, what Shakespeare's poem had indicated, that the lovers died without issue. But on the main matter there was accord—between these two persons being honored in this symbolic way there existed love of an extraordinary quality, and their union was to be thought of as evidence of incorruptible perfection.

All these poets were deep in philosophy, and in particular were well acquainted with Platonic thought. But even allowing for what we know of their congeniality, the reader is bound to be impressed by the sophistication with which they all brought philosophy to bear in making use of the legend of the phoenix. As Bernard Newdigate observed in his edition of the poems, it would be a mistake to interpret Shakespeare's apart from its setting. And then, it turns out, when we do examine the speculations of Marston and Chapman and Jonson we are the better prepared to appreciate Sidney Lanier's remark, that Shakespeare's poem 'has more complex ideas in it, word for word, than perhaps any other poem in our language'.[3]

Shakespeare's poem tells of a ceremony held before an urn holding the ashes of the Phoenix and Turtle. The poems of Marston that immediately follow are introduced in such a way as to suggest they form a sequence: 'A narration and description of a most exact wondrous creature, arising out of the Phoenix and Turtle Doues ashes.' The first words seem to be referring to Shakespeare's poem:

> O twas a mouing *Epicidium!*
> Can Fire? can Time? can blackest Fate consume
> So rare creation? No; tis thwart to sence,
> Corruption quakes to touch such excellence,
> Nature exclaimes for Iustice, Iustice Fate,
> Ought into nought can neuer remigrate.

But soon we see that the rejoinder is to be much more than that, it is to be a quite extensive and even labored expatiation in philosophy, and whether Marston meant it to pursue further or to correct the ideas on immortality he found in Shakespeare's poem, he developed his expostulations in what appears to be all seriousness.

His first poem continues in elaborating the praise of the two lovers. It carries forward the idea of a spiritual issue of the

marriage, developing what from one aspect are hyperboles into
sober philosophic meanings:

> what glorious issue (brighter
> Then clearest fire, and beyond faith farre whiter
> Then *Dians* tier) now springs from yonder flame?
> Let me stand numb'd with wonder, neuer came
> So strong amazement on astonish'd eie
> As this, this measureless pure Raritie.
> Lo now; th'xtracture of deuinest *Essence*,
> The Soul of heauens labour'd *Quintessence*,
> (*Peans* to *Phoebus*) from deare Louer's death,
> Takes sweet creation and all blessing breath.
> . . . of this same *Metaphisicall*,
> God, Man, nor Woman, but elix'd of all
> My labouring thoughts, with strained ardor sing.

The thoughts Marston is developing became somewhat clearer
when in the beginning lines of the next poem, which is called
'The description of this Perfection,' he asks,

> Dares then thy too audacious sense
> Presume, define that boundlesse *Ens*,
> That amplest thought transcendeth?

Evidently we are to relate this love and the issue of it to metaphysics, to the idea of a realm of being in which there are none of
the limitations known in the material world, and in which beauty
and perfection live eternally, uncorrupted:

> Diuinest Beautie? that was slightest,
> That adorn'd this wondrous Brightest,
> Which had nought to be corrupted.
> In this, Perfection had no meane
> To this, Earths purest was vncleane
> Which vertue euen instructed.
> By it all Beings deck'd and stained,
> *Ideas* that are idly fained
> Onely here subsist inuested.

> Dread not to giue strain'd praise at all,
> No speech is Hyperbolicall,
> To this perfection blessed.[4]

However, it is in the next poem, 'Perfectioni Hymnus', that Marston in continuing the reasoning offers the key to that feature of the Stoic philosophy he is expounding. He asks a number of questions—what are we to call this perfection?

> Call it Perfection? Fie
> Tis perfecter then brightest names can light it.

The questions continue until there is an apparently satisfactory answer:

> Deepe Contemplations wonder?
> That appellation giue this excellence.
> Within all best confin'd,
> (Now feebler *Genius* end thy slighter riming)
> No Suburbes all is *Mind*
> As farre from spot, as possible defining.

In the margin Marston supplied a note: 'Differentia Deorum & hominum (apud Senecam) sic habet nostri melior pars animus in illis nulla pars extra animum.' By thus referring to the incapacity of the finite human mind to grasp the infinite, Marston indicates that this newly formed spirit now participates in the world of perfect being, 'that boundless *Ens*'; that he is regarding the love of those two mortal creatures as attaining an immortal existence in the divine realm from which in the first instance they were derived. We are thus taken back to that early line—

> Ought into nought can neuer remigrate.

We may judge something of the density of his reasoning when we turn to the passage in Seneca Marston is referring to. 'Here the soul learns what it has long sought to know, it begins to know God. What is God? The mind of the universe. What is God? He is everything that you see and everything you do not see. His magnitude is such that nothing can be imagined that is greater. He is all things to himself. He works from within and without.

What is the difference between God's nature and ours? The mind is but the better part of us, in him there is nothing that is not mind. All is reason.' (*Quaestiones Naturales*, I[V], 13-4).[5]

Seneca is here speaking of God as a creator, and he thinks of God creating as an artist does, following a conception in His mind. In the so-called Platonic Letters to Lucilius (LVIII and LXV) we see even more clearly what Marston has been absorbing. When he tells of 'Ideas that . . . onely here subsist inuested' he seems to be pursuing the reasoning of Seneca on these *exemplaria* of all things that God's mind contains: '"What are these?" you ask. They are Plato's own furniture, so to speak; he calls them "ideas", and from them all visible things are created, and according to their pattern all things are fashioned. They are immortal, unchangeable, inviolable. And this "idea", or rather, Plato's conception of it, is as follows: "The idea is the everlasting pattern of those things which are created by nature."' (LVIII, 15-19) Furthermore: 'God has within himself these patterns of all things, and his mind comprehends the harmonies and the measures of the whole totality of things which are to be carried out; he is filled with these shapes which Plato calls the "ideas"—imperishable, unchangeable, not subject to decay. And therefore, though men die, humanity itself, or the idea of man, according to which man is moulded, lasts on, and though men toil and perish, it suffers no change.' (LXV, 7-8).

It is in the fifty-eighth letter (6) that there is Seneca's single use of the term *essentia*, which he apologizes for as a translation of the Greek *ousia*, but the signification is vital to him: 'natura continens fundamentum omnium.' Marston's 'boundlesse Ens' may not be strictly faithful to Senecas's meaning but it is like it in supplying the sense of ultimate reference. Here Seneca was trying to come to grips with a question in which Plato and Aristotle differ, and in speaking of ideas as subsisting in God's mind he seems to be attempting to reconcile Aristotle's concept of immanent forms with Plato's concept of transcendent ideas.[6] And this is precisely what Marston believes he is resolving.

In both letters Seneca expatiates on the moral that in the midst of all that is mortal and that decays the wise man gives his mind to the imperishable, that which is not 'stained', as Marston says. Here Seneca does not speak of perfection as such nor of beauty, although he is concerned with goodness and above all else with what is immortal. It is this that Marston is making most of, the immortal life of the offspring of the dead birds. He conceives of this as a 'quintessential' form that has come into being through the union of their souls. That form appears to be what has existed from eternity in the mind of God, what has come into being through Him and what returns to Him. The lovers in their deaths that give occasion to this new forming are now participating in the Mind that is all in all, that is All.[7]

Platonists and scholastics alike point to the inadequacies in this reasoning, and Shakespeare's poem will, I believe, avoid such, but Marston appears to be content with Seneca's presentation of the Stoic system. In his verses there is so little suggestion of personal immortality or of divine intercession or of incarnation that one may not confidently extend the interpretation in giving either a more precisely Platonic or Christian coloring to his meaning. In contrast with this inchoate, what we may call undeveloped, Platonizing we are able to see how much more complexly articulated are the meanings in Shakespeare's poem that Marston may suppose he is refining.

Of all the contributors to this collection Chapman was of course the most given to expounding philosophy, and in the poem he wrote for this occasion he seems to take for granted his readers' acquaintance with what might otherwise call for more expounding, for much more elaborate notes than Marston's supplied. With almost no preparation he develops his accustomed reasoning on the union of souls that constant love effects, and the translation that follows upon that, into a psychology of art and a description of the effect upon the poet himself of this admirable lady the Turtle represents:

She was to him th'*Analisde* World of pleasure,
    Her firmenesse cloth'd him in varietie;

Excesse of all things, he ioyd in her measure,
  Mourn'd when she mourn'd, and dieth when she dies.
Like him I bound th'instinct of all my powres,
  In her that bounds the Empire of desert,
And Time nor Change (that all things else deuoures,
  But truth eterniz'd in a constant heart)
Can change me more from her, then her from merit,
That is my forme, and giues my being spirit.

His central idea is that love takes to itself what it loves, and in loving what is good the lover is enriched. Just as the Phoenix, loving the Turtle, not what was mortal in her, what was changing, but what was steadfast, virtue, took greater strength and greater richness from her wealth and constancy, just so the poet, admiring this creature, finds in her what gives measure and form to his love and life to his very being. Just so the heart devoted to truth becomes eternal with the eternity of truth. Knowledge and love become one.[8] The wealth of the tradition of thought Chapman is drawing upon we shall see more of when we look closely at Shakespeare's poem but here it may be enough only to notice the application of the Neo-Platonic idea that the mind in contemplating takes on the form and life of what it contemplates.

Jonson's poems are somewhat more expansive than Chapman's, less so than Marston's, but characteristically they are direct, explicit, and supported by as thoroughly disciplined speculation as Shakespeare's. One of the poems he contributed, *Epos*, commences in demanding that we exclude from our thought any idea that the love of these two was carnal—it was not the 'blind Desire' that in the world at large is called Love, rather—

                                    true *Loue*
        No such effects doth proue:
    That is an *Essence* most gentile, and fine.
        Pure, perfect; nay diuine:
    It is a golden Chaine let down from Heauen,
        Whose linkes are bright, and euen
    That fals like Sleepe on Louers; and combines

25

The soft and sweetest *Minds*
In equal knots: This beares no *Brands* nor *Darts*
To murder different harts,
But in a calme and God-like vnitie,
Preserues *Communitie*.

He is thus characterizing a union brought about by a divine power, joining 'Minds', which seems to mean that which is most refined, most spirit-like, everlastingly, we suppose, and changelessly.

The figure of a gold chain let down from Heaven comes from Homer, and Jonson cited this as a source as well as the *Theataetus* in a gloss he supplied to the *Hymenaei*. In this same note he provided also an elaborate allegorical interpretation from Macrobius. In short, here is more Platonizing. And the note is worth quoting, I think, if only to stress the congeniality of spirit in which these poets were making their contributions to this memorial. 'Mentioned by *Homer Ilia*. Θ which many haue interpreted diuersely: al [*sic*] Allegorically, *Pla. in Th* (*e*) *æteto*, vnderstands it to be the *Sunne*, (with) which while he circles the world in his course, all things are safe, and preserued: others vary it. *Macrob.* (to whose interpretation I am specially affected in my Allusion) considers it thus: *in Som. Scip. libr.* 1 *cap.* 14. [Accordingly, since Mind emanates from the Supreme God and Soul from Minds, and Mind, indeed, forms and suffuses all below with life, and since this is the one splendor lighting up everything and visible in all, like a countenance reflected in many mirrors arranged in a row, and since all follow on in continuous succession, degenerating step by step in their downward course, the close observer will find that from the Supreme God even to the bottommost dregs of the universe there is one tie, binding at every link and never broken. This is the golden chain of Homer which, he tells us, God ordered to hang down from the sky to the earth.]' (W. H. Stahl).[9]

Jonson completes the note: 'To which strength and euennesse of connexion, I haue not absurdly likened this vniting of *Humours*, and *Affections*, by the sacred *Powers* of *Marriage*'. Such is the 'God-like Communitie' he had in mind.

Reducing the gist of the contributions of these poets to a few words, one might say that Marston was chiefly exploring the idea of participation in eternal being; Chapman is taking account of something like 'the marriage of true minds', with the further consideration that love is a particular factor in bringing the human into touch with the divine; and Jonson is especially interested in the descent and the ascent of the soul. The ideas of each are obviously part and parcel of the thought of the others.

Shakespeare's poem owes its power in part to the richness and variety of the poetic conventions fused in a form representing the preparation of a funeral: the medieval conceits of the bird-mass and of parliaments of fowls; hyperboles from the poetry of courtly and romantic love; symbols from ancient legends; suggestions of the ancient and medieval 'complaints of nature' assimilated to the manner of liturgy. But the power as the beauty depend almost equally on the skill with which, through the barest of language and deceptively bald statements, metaphysical issues are raised and resolved.

We learn from the beginning verses, at first indirectly, that two birds have died, their love for each other in some sense the instrument of their deaths, for it was this that consumed them in 'a mutuall flame'. The air of celebration appropriate to the rite suggests that love was not so much the cause of the deaths of bodies as of the freeing and transformation of souls.

Certain birds are invited by name to join in the rite, others are enjoined from appearing. After the summoning and the invocation there is an anthem in which the nature of the love that bound these two is represented, chiefly expressed in the language of philosophy and theology, the assertions so flatly made they must be accepted as precisely meant. In the concluding Threnos a figure identified as Reason confesses its incapacity to comprehend what is happening, although it supposes Love is able to. Reason nevertheless sings a dirge, explaining, as it had not been explained before, the nature of the life and death of the two the requiem is honoring, and ends in bidding those present, and all who would join them, to pray for the dead:

> To this urne let those repaire,
> That are either true or faire,
> For these dead Birds, sigh a prayer.

A succession of assertions and paradoxes has told us that in their loves and in their deaths each of the two has at once lost and preserved his individual being. In the steadily increasing complexity of the ideas sustaining these claims the images of birds consumed with fire and of their ashes and of the urn dissolve as we try to conceive of a union of selves that transcends the limits reason and the senses place on our imagining. We are left in the end rapt by the appeal of the conception, invited to share in the hopes of those who remain in life, not only such birds who are the fit symbols and sponsors of devotion, but all humans as well who in the dignity of faithfulness and beauty wish a like end for themselves, praying before a monument to the power rewarding love with rest.

Reducing the substance of the poem to so limited a summary we see plainly how much the paradoxical and the preposterous require of metaphysics if the sense of seriousness with which all is being uttered is to be justified. And metaphysics employed responsibly as we are told that a certain attachment in love attests to a miraculous power.

The initial circumstance is the key one—it is humans, not birds, we are learning of, persons so joined in sympathy we may not think of them as ever to be separated. They inhabited two bodies, and yet, in death as in life, it seems, they remain united. Each looked upon the other and into the other's eyes—

> So betweene them Love did shine.

Seeing love each saw itself. The words that say this are at once flat assertions and oracular. There is in them something of the manner of occult speech, for the reader is left to figure for himself the stages through which what has happened has taken place.

Each sees, we judge, what it recognizes as itself loving and being loved, at one and the same timeless instant disappearing and finding itself in the minglings of sight, an unceasing and as it were a growing exchange. Intent with love, sight ceases to be sight and becomes love, and in this transformation, this splendor and illumination, the lovers lose the sense of themselves, they feel the loss of self as it would seem to be if annihilated by fire, yet in fact there is no loss for not even what one might call solitary in the self is destroyed since it rediscovers itself in the other:

> So betweene them Love did shine,
> That the *Turtle* saw his right,
> Flaming in the *Phœnix* sight;
> Either was the others mine.

There is continuous, exultant gain, each forever discovering new wealth.[10]

The Turtle, seeing himself possessed by what he knows as love, has no care for himself any longer, nor does the Phoenix care to remain only herself, to survive alone. In some sense each ceases to be its own and yet each is now another self—the language of paradox is inescapable—neither owns itself nor, on the other hand, is owned by the other for each is being preserved even as it is being destroyed. Although reason would say that the bodies were separated yet the sense of even that separation is lost in the sense of gain. Both reason and language acknowledge their shortcomings in affirming the miraculous.

A single assertion is not enough so the summoner to the rite and the Anthem continue with still others that bring into the conception more and more extensive meaning:

> Propertie was thus appalled,
> That the selfe was not the same:
> Single Natures double name,
> Neither two nor one was called.

A personification, an allusion to philosophic doctrine, a paradox, ring changes upon the same idea in order to lead feeling into such sympathy with thought that we shall be led to agree that love can indeed escape the confinements of time and space and come into another order of existence.

The suggestion of astonishment, the sense of wordlessness in 'appalled', signifies that philosophy will be tested to the limit to account for this, and so we are prepared to be brought into the almost innumerable paths of speculation philosophy and theology have prepared. In the end, however, it will be the ghost-like images, the movement of the verse, the half-plaintive half-exultant tone, the continuous evocation of wonder in the face of what is so curiously explained, that will support the thought with conviction. The images that are only on the verge of taking shape, the almost monotone chant with its rising pitch, the rhythms so dominant they recall 'the blessed mutter of the mass'—all this to carry us along into an acceptance of the preposterous in every sense. The meaning almost breaks free from the words but the intricacies of the reasoning as much as the strangeness of the circumstances hold us so intently and yet as it were confusedly that we all but overlook Reason's calling attention to itself. The illusion that images are about to take form, the limit set to the harmonies, the narrow range of the pitch, hold us so strangely we are persuaded to take nonsense for sense, contradiction as resolution, wordlessness as the testimony for wonder, the laboring of reason as its own disqualification—the whole justifying the faith. The apprehension of another in loving, this is the reality. The verse will re-create the state, the thought will accentuate it. The but partly seen figuring, the efforts of logic, the suggestion of incantation, are succeeding in doing what they do for Plato—as in the allegory of the cave, all that is elusive or obscure is emphasized in order to help us know about light: 'La nuit de la contradiction est en effet plus libératrice que toutes les évidences positives.'[11] Antithesis, contradiction, paradox, even, perhaps, the *coincidentia oppositorum*.

The repetitions, but no more than the variations, like the sounding of changes suggest endless enumeration, and the wealth of them emphasizes the irony in the preposterousness of paying such honor to the ashes of birds. And that irony in turn leads into the sense that is anything but preposterous or susceptible of exaggeration—the purity at the heart of love.

There is a sense in which the state of the lovers is to be spoken of as ecstasy. The poem is not, however, the expression of the lovers themselves but of someone, knowing the state of these two, who is giving witness to it. And more, much as Chapman said of himself in contemplating the state of the lovers, his own spirit was given a new life. Again the techniques of irony are counted on to achieve by indirection what ecstatic utterance would tell if it could. And there is irony again in the technical terminology used not to describe but to communicate the sense of the state it was invented only to describe. Thus by all such devices, but above all by the treatment of the relationship of the Phoenix and Turtle as of that nature that reason cannot comprehend, the poem works to show that the idea of infinite satisfaction is justified.

The poem will hardly let us put it down. It achieves its success through such almost unintelligible means that it requires to be pored over. There are puzzles to be solved but there are also other demands—we need to know why the paradoxes follow in their particular succession, why there should be a breaking-off where there is, and why a figure called Reason should be brought in to take over—

> Reason in it selfe confounded,
> Saw Division grow together.

And so we, similarly at a loss, yet as persuaded as Reason of what it saw increasing, persuaded that the contradictions express truths, are held so intently we recognize in our very attention a power like that ascribed to love, the power to free the spirit from constraint.

The figures that at first seemed hardly more than artifice and calculation—

> Number there in love was slaine—

the language of love talking to itself, are presenting us with a universe conceived to be without dimension, a realm of being thought is able to conceive of although imagination cannot. The abstract words, the contradictions and oppositions, speak with perfect assurance in denying what our senses as well as reason tell us. Statement after statement points to a conception of the ground and substance of reality, of what underlies appearances. It is a conception at once like and unlike Marston's and Seneca's 'natura continens fundamentum omnium', for imaging would misrepresent it. So there is the recourse to paradox and to abstractions as bodiless as may be to acquaint us with a sense of the very quality of what is alone real, of Being.

The paradoxes have their own logic, they open up into a metaphysics reason is able to entertain, or believes it is. At every step we are being reminded that our idea of what is limited depends upon an idea of the limitless, our ideas of number and of space to that which is without quantity and dimension. All, in short, provokes us with our capacity to entertain the thought of the infinite and eternal.

This is the capacity Saint Anselm argued for in affirming the existence of God, the value of the conception of the perfect as the means of the measurement of the finite and the mortal. In this poem, love in uniting persons represents a limitless power. That limitlessness is also the character of truth and beauty—

> Beautie, Truth, and Raritie,
> Grace in all simplicitie—

Taken with truth and beauty humans share in their limitless life.

In this partial recapitulation I have only briefly alluded to the philosophic and theological meanings that underly the paradoxes, individually and in relation to each other. The authority of the poem depends greatly upon the fullness of the meanings that do in fact sustain an argument. Ideas of being and transcendence are drawn on, the idea of incarnation seems not to be excluded. But however complex the thought, another marvel is not so much in the economy as in the bareness of the language and the boldness of the rhythms that establish the character of unintermitted celebration. The very complexity of the conventions, literary and terminological, by their coherence communicates the integrity of devotion which neither logic nor images disrupt. What Saint Bernard said was true of ecstasy of another order applies to this: 'to meditate upon truth and not to have it clothed in material images pertains to angelic purity.'[12] At the start the images were as indispensable as the bodies themselves in which love took rise but in the communication of the increasing strength to the union, images and reasoning alike fade out.

Commencing in the imperative mode—

Let the bird of lowdest lay—

the announcement of the rite tells something of the order that is to be followed. A speaker distinguishes the participants and indicates the parts of the service and the forms—invocation, anthem, threnos. Most is spoken, or chanted, as it were by the director of the rite—it is he who calls for the introductory hymn, afterwards indicating the entrance and chanting of the priest, calling upon the mourning congregation for their participation, making way for the summation of Reason at the end after the ashes are deposited in the urn.

The directness and bareness is deceptive for the ceremony indicates a wealth of spectacle as well as of thought and passion. Like the simple namings in incantations, the words are the distillations of an enormous burden, bare but with the suggestions of the occult, and the elusive images are yet known to be the traces of a splendid rite.

All is overlaid also with a complex of ironies. We are supposed to be attending a mass of birds celebrating the miraculous death of other birds while we are thinking of the death of two extraordinary humans and the celebrants who are exulting in their translation to eternal rest. The fictional rite—fanciful, grotesque, decorous—is devised to engender that order of contemplation in which neither fiction nor fancy has any part, the contemplation of splendor and peace.

Another impression derives from the multiple character of the poem as a summoning to prayer, as a series of glosses upon the ceremony, as the repetition of an actual lament, and as a description and a narration. The passing back and forth from the directions given by the leader—

Let the bird of lowdest lay—

to the hymn itself, then to an unidentified narrator, and finally to the interruption of Reason and the Threnos, all has the effect of fastening our attention upon the one who is managing this succession. In the first instance we become aware of the one who is directing the service without participating in it, and in the next, to the unidentified narrator, the only one we come to think of to be in a position to put it all together, the poet himself. In Jean de Condé's *Messe des Oiseaux* it is Venus who summons the birds to the mass. The initiator, the manager, in Shakespeare's poem is not identified, but it appears that as the master of ceremonies his purpose is to arrange for the glorification and to establish the manner of its proceeding. As for the one who tells all this in a poem, it can only be that he does so in order to underwrite its authenticity. A similarly complex conception is evident in the conclusion of the *De Planctu Naturae* of Alain de Lille. 'Genius', in the vestments of a priest, 'called out from the secret places of his mind' his final determination. Until now the work has been offered as the record of a vision, but now, it has been observed, 'Alain's abstracted hero exists finally on a transcendent level above and beyond the cosmos defined by the aesthetic structure of the poem.' He speaks now 'by the authority of the Absolute Being'.[13] *The Phœnix and Turtle* ends with the words of an unnamed speaker calling out of the poem for the readers themselves to join in the prayer, by the authority of his own illumination.

The ironies are all but inexhaustible. Worshippers at a requiem in life are of course aware that a form has been prepared for them and they know that in the ordering of the antiphons and responses a refined wisdom is inducting them into communal prayer. They are also, of course, full of the sense of the particular occasion and of the service the language is providing for their grief and joy. They understand that the traditional words exclude something of the note of individuality, as choric utterance must, but in exchange the words of the liturgy embody the generic passion that tradition sanctifies as the quintessential. But the rite in this poem—or rather, the reporting of it—offers in place of the traditional sanctity the delights of novelty and wildness. The known forms are changed into a ritual performed by birds, interrupted by a most unexpected participant, Reason, who ends the ceremony with a deferential invitation to a whole other world of mourners—the readers of the poem—to join in a prayer.

The director of the rite, presenting it as a composition of his own, thereby becomes also a narrator apart from the ritual. As if at the very moment he is summoning the persons to participate he is standing apart, contemplating the completed action. Our sense of him as an observer voids the sense of the immediate passions, while our sense of him as a participant in the ceremony leads us to concentrate with him upon the world he is contemplating. We, the readers, those the narrator has in mind, are also being led by the paradoxes to concentrate so intently upon the argument and upon its end that our mind and spirit are engaged as near as may be to what the Phoenix and Turtle know—a state we may speak of in a traditional manner as one we know of even if we have not ourselves known the thing itself. We do not demur when the poem speaks at one and the same time of the death of the two birds as having taken place and as still in process.[14]

Mourners in life, following the progression of a rite, are all the while reflecting on the form that has been prepared for them in helping them sustain existence. They do so the more religiously for having known those who are dead and because the service has the authority of centuries. But here the service never quite takes form, we never know for whom it is being performed, and besides, it is fantastic. Yet even so we are brought as close as words are able to to sympathy with mystical transport. We are brought to this as we sense the state of the writer of the poem who is leading us to follow the transformations with his mind and as it were with his sight. We follow him as his thought contemplates what true union must be. We follow him in the suggestions of a rite, through the labyrinth of the logic that is developed in order to confound sense, past the barriers set by reason. We tolerate the off-key pitch, the rhythm of the half-sleeping consciousness, lulled, and finally enthralled. Enthralled as if taken up in the consciousness of the poet himself as he becomes absorbed in what it means that selves have been exchanged. Our own thoughts recognize in him the fullness of awe, the one who is not only outside the ceremony, remaining also apart from us.

The thought occurs to us that the poem took occasion from actual love and actual deaths and that we might be making still something else of this if we knew who these persons were, or if the birds are taken to represent abstractions and not persons, or if we should all the while be thinking of the relations of the members of the Trinity. But I think none or all these identifications would substantially qualify the character of the poem as an oblique representation of the poet's remembrance of an estatic moment in his life. It seems right to apply to this poem Dante's words from the thirty-third canto of the *Inferno*—'As he who is dreaming seeth, and when the dream is gone the passion stamped remaineth, and nought else cometh to the mind again; for almost wholly faileth me my vision, yet doth the sweetness that was born of it still drip within my heart.' *The Phœnix and Turtle* is no effort to communicate such ecstasy as Dante himself undertakes to re-create in us in the last cantos of the *Divine Comedy*, but it is, I think, an index to such a vision.

In the *Paradiso* when Dante speaks of his vision, looking directly upon God, he says it is an experience he can no longer remember yet he retains the conviction of its authority. More, too, remains, of course, enough to permit him to order the entire *Commedia*, and in its culmination to re-create that authority, even, it seems, the authority of the vision. He appears, despite what he has said, to succeed in communicating the ineffable. *The Phœnix and Turtle* communicates no such blinding power we know in Dante's verses but it does express feeling and thought sustained so powerfully that we can very well refer to an experience for which the word *flame* is precisely the right one. It would be wrong to attempt to argue that Shakespeare's subsequent writing sprang so centrally from this as Dante's composition. But it would be remiss in considering the matters touched on metaphysically in *A Midsummer Night's Dream* and *Julius Caesar* and *Hamlet* and *The Tempest* without making reference to reasoning so packed as in this consideration of a love. We know very well how shifting the lights are that shine through *Hamlet*, for example, how spirituality and skepticism and impiety mingle in marvellous richness. Although in that play there is a mention of the Christian Incarnation that Professor W. M. Merchant has spoken of as the loveliest in all the plays[15]—

> Some say that ever, 'gainst that season comes
> Wherein our Saviour's birth is celebrated,
> This bird of dawning singeth all night long—
> $\qquad$ (*Hamlet*, I.1.158–160)

there is also quite as vivid a sense of death as a peaceful or else a haunted sleep. But seeing what has been presented in *The Phœnix and Turtle* we can only suppose that if our last interpretation of the tragedy of Hamlet is to be the conclusion of despair, it must be the despair of an author who has forgotten or renounced the vision.

As for *The Tempest*—again in all but random illustration—if we should accept its final burden as the resignation of a Stoic, for whom the magnificent images of men's minds are always returning to the bosom of the *anima mundi*, that conclusion too would signify a loss of faith in such felicity where, in Plotinus as well as in Saint Paul, the individual soul absorbed in the love of the One yet remains itself.

II

Love's Labour's Lost ends in an elegant spectacle, two richly ornate half-birds, half-gods, singing two of the most beautiful songs in the world. *The Phœnix and Turtle*, so much more intricate in intellectuality, is as ornate but even richer and more mannered, making us think of the splendid creatures in Nicholas Hillyard's miniatures and Jones's masques. The high-lights and the strong contrasts, the miraculous and glorious Phoenix and the scavengers, the promises lighting up death, the sub-human world and spirits, a wonderful procession of ghostly creatures passing in mock stateliness, the music, grave in pace, though in a minor key. Then the first words—

Let the bird of lowdest lay—

strangely allusive, set the tone. The ceremony for burial that traditionally never invites criticism here demands to be noticed for the artifice.

The thought in the marriage songs of the Owl and the Cuckoo is rich enough but the funeral lyric carries still more complex thought. We may think we are being shown one of the styles of the high Renaissance tested to discover if it is equal to the piety that the romanesque and the Gothic had embodied in serving the sacrament of the funeral rites of Christians. The poem proceeds, of course, as a succession of stages in time but the language tells of an event neither in act nor completed. It is as if the words are meant only to form the picture of a moment, like one of those funeral statues fixing in ironic solidity the translation of bodies and the hovering of angels. And indeed I think we are to regard the poem as the representation of an arrested moment, which is also to say that it is the celebration of the continuing present as it tells of the union of those resting 'to eternitie'.

Many of the words of Shakespeare's poem belong to terminology that has its uses not only in scholasticism but in the Creeds and prayer books. Some of the same words were in use in the 'Platonic theology' and in devotional and mystical writings. One verse moves into another in making precise discriminations among their meanings, and we may detect in what seems at first a statement of generally Platonic import a modification of Aristotle's or a further qualification of Aquinas's, or Ficino's. But even as we find ourselves compelled to accommodate the possible meanings of 'distincts' and 'Divisions' and 'Propertie' and 'essence'[16] and the others we are all the while as much drawn to consider what the words bring with them from their uses in poetry and in mystical writings. They are being used to characterize a remarkable love and the state of the union of two lovers, on earth, and in heaven it seems, and they fit with conceptions we are acquainted with in the poets of the *dolce stil nuovo*, in the troubadours, even in those following the Platonists of the School of Chartres. So, briefly, in Dante:

> Feremi nel cor sempre la tua luce,
> Comme raggio in la stella,
> Poichè l'anima mia fu fatta ancella
> Della tua podestà primieramenta. (*Canzone* ix. 16–9)

> Upon my heart thy light doth ever strike, as
> on a star the ray, since when my soul became the
> handmaiden of thy power at the first. (Wicksteed)

> In lei s'accoglie d'ogni beltà luce:
> Perchè negli occhi sì bella mi luce,
> Quando io la miro, chi'io la veggio in pietra,
> E poi in altro ov' io volga mia luce. (*Sestina* ii. 37–42)

> In her is gathered all beauty's light; . . .
> wherefore in my eyes so beauteous does she shine,
> when I look on her, that I see her in the rock,
> and then wheresoever else I turn my sight. (Wicksteed)

Professor A. H. Fairchild points to something of the richness in the conception of this poem that belongs also to the poetry of courtly love.[17] But apart from many certifiable sources for Shakespeare's thought and the manner of the poem there is the more general consideration of the ways in which not only conventions but traditional ideas and meanings came to him. Platonism, we can be sure, he met with as much or more in the poetry and fiction of the Middle Ages and his own century as in treatises. Often this would have been diluted or distorted, but the nature of his mind was such that it calls for the kind of comment Professor John Burnet made in interpreting a reference to the music of the spheres in *The Merchant of Venice*: 'The School of Chartres was the legitimate successor of Plato's Academy, and its teaching was based on the work of Chalcidius. . . . It is in [Bernard Silvester] that personified Nature makes her appearance practically for the first time. Then comes the *De planctu naturae* of Alan of Lille, to whom Chaucer [in *The Parliament of Fowles*] refers his readers for a description of the goddess Nature, and from whom he borrows her designation as 'God's vicar general.' . . . It is a probable conjecture that Shakespeare's Platonism first came to him from sources of this kind.' And then, as Burnet went on to disentangle the references to cosmic harmony, he concluded that Shakespeare had discovered the essential in the midst of the elaborations: 'Shakespeare has picked out the pure gold from the dross with an unerring instinct. The Aristotelean and Scholastic accretions which disfigured the doctrine have all dropped away, and the thought of Pythagoras stands revealed in its original simplicity.'[18] Burnet believed he was able to perceive in the sense of 'the muddy vesture of decay', thought so clearly formed it corresponded with the original inspiration of the traditions and conventions Shakespeare perforce depended on. I think we are also able to say of the conceits and conventions that have gone into *The Phœnix and Turtle*—derived from whatever antecedents—that they bring into view the thoughts of the analogous originals in their full authority.

Shakespeare is celebrating that order of love of which it is said that two lovers become each other even while remaining themselves. In a certain elementary way this is how friends commonly talk, and when Cicero has Cato remark that his friend was 'another self' we understand this is how everyone speaks when conscious his friend sees and feels as he does.

The language is often the same whether it is love or friendship that is spoken of, and immemorially the reasoning of Socrates and Plato is brought forward to provide the authority sympathy of this kind appears to deserve. There enter then all those considerations that make it seem wise to conceive of body and soul to be separable only in a limited sense, and to consider the soul, or the soul joined to the body, to be the person, and to be immortal.[19] And so in friendship that which is capable of union is said to merge with its fellow, and eternally.

The language used to tell of this—as in the word 'merge'—inevitably falsifies the conception, lending to the spiritual the dimensions that belong to the material. There were to be throughout history innumerable efforts to discover other figurings—of bodies dissolved in liquid, of water in wine, of the mingling of air and light, the merging of flames—to characterize such a union.[20] But whether through the nature of the imagination or of language, the idea of something occupying space crowds into the conception to threaten to falsify what is thought to be without dimension and possessing unending life.[21]

Aristotle understood as well as Cato how much friendship was to be valued but he was bound to qualify the Platonic claims. He, too, was agreeable to such phrases as 'a friend is another self', but in his sense this would signify an identity of interest and concern and not an identity of persons or of souls: 'The good man grieves and rejoices, more than any other, with himself; for the same thing is always painful, and the same thing always pleasant, and not one thing at one time and another at another; for he has, so to speak, nothing to repent of. Therefore, since each of these characteristics belongs to the good man in relation to himself, and he is related to his friend as to himself (for his friend is another self), friendship too is thought to be one of these attributes, and those who have these attributes to be friends.' (*Ethics*, IX, 4–1166a)

There could hardly be anyone who valued friendship more than Saint Augustine, and his phrase for a friend—*dimidium animae suae* (*Confessions*, IV, 6)—returns us to the Platonic sense of that love which unites souls and which leads to one of the formulations—Saint Bernard's—that is at the heart of the Christian way of harmonizing the Platonic understanding with Christian faith and philosophy: 'Neque enim praesentior spiritus noster est ubi animat, quam ubi amat.'[22] And in the long history that gave Petrarch and those following him such rich conceptions with which to proclaim the authority lovers could appeal to in professing the completeness of their union there is the special emphasis on the mutuality of the relationship that Christianity made so much of, and, for that matter, often independently of that, the troubadours as well. Among many uses of the idea in the Middle Ages Professor Perella singled out this of Bernart de Ventadorn:

> Lady, if I were but heard by you as earnestly as I wish to show you, at the start of our love we would exchange spirits. Thereby a clever wit would be bestowed upon me; for then I would know your affairs and you mine, equally, and we would from two hearts be made one.'[23]

So in Shakespeare, where so little of the imagery is concrete, there yet is this—

> Hearts remote, yet not asunder.

There is Petrarch's:

> So della mia nemica cercar l'orme,
> E temer trovarla; e so in qual guisa
> L'amante nell'amato si trasforme.
> (*Trionfo d'Amore*, III, 160–2)

> I trod the paths made happy by her feet,
> And search the foe I am afraid to meet.
> I know how lovers metamorphosed are
> To that they love. (Hume)

The same idea governs Michael Angelo's sonnet, 'It is with your bright eyes I see.' It pervades Leonardo's thought: 'The lover moves towards the thing loved as the sense and the sensible and joins with it and makes itself into one and the same thing.... When the lover is joined with the beloved, there it rests.'[24]

No single psychological or philosophical reference may illustrate the variety of meanings the conceit has encompassed, and in Shakespeare's writing alone one may discover that it expresses the most serious and sustained reasoning and also the most fanciful flirting.

The Comedy of Errors is wonderfully lighthearted, and in it there is some of the usual playing about with the then fashionable Petrarchan and Platonizing ways of courting. Antipholus of Syracuse has been enchanted by the siren-like beauty of the sister of the wife of his twin—

> It is thyself, mine own self's better part,
> Mine eye's clear eye, my dear heart's dearer heart,
> My food, my fortune, and my sweet hope's aim,
> My sole earth's heaven, and my heaven's claim.
>
> (III. ii. 61–4)

Luciana, having every reason to believe he means to deceive her, thinking this to be the other twin and her sister's husband, tries to put him off—

> All this my sister is, or else should be— (65)

which only leads him to turn the conceit inside out—

> Call thyself sister, sweet, for I am thee. (66)

The paradoxes that in *The Phœnix and Turtle* are used in preparing a requiem are the matter of the most playful love-making in Ephesus. Yet even here they open on to tragic prospects, and in later works the failure of love will be referred to the inconceivable, the divorce of those who believed they were united in just such a sense. So Troilus can only say that what has taken place could not:

> Within my soul there doth conduce a fight
> Of this strange nature, that a thing inseparate
> Divides more wider than the sky and earth,
> And yet the spacious breadth of this division
> Admits no orifex for a point as subtle
> As Ariachne's broken woof to enter.
>
> (V. ii. 145–50)

Thus from the beginning in Shakespeare's writing we observe

the wealth of meaning the idea serves, and later as well we see in the confidence that now this character in the plays, now that, places in such sympathy just such prospects for suffering and disillusion as illuminate this early play—

> Against my soul's pure truth why labour you
> To make it wander in an unknown field?—
> (*The Comedy of Errors*, III. ii. 37–8)

The lovely words are lightly offered but they are rich with visions of suffering and holiness. 'The Tragique Scene' the mourners contemplate in *The Phœnix and Turtle* was already taking form in the thoughts of the lovers of the farcical comedy. What might have been, to begin with, the charm of a fashion, was to reveal such seriousness as called for the support of philosophy and religion.

In such expressions we are in fact meeting with meanings of central importance to the *Phaedrus*, to the *Vita Nuova*, to *The Celestial Hierarchies*. In the force they have for Shakespeare they manifest the freshness and profundity we know in their original forms, as authentically as the idea of the harmony of the spheres makes itself known in *The Merchant of Venice*.

Socrates in the *Symposium* told how Zeus in the far distant past had divided men into two, and thereafter the parts wandered about looking for each other. In what has been spoken of, I think not improperly, as a marvellous joke, Aristophanes tells how, when the re-union was effected, the two are caught up in the amazement of love. 'And Hephaestus once spoke to two who were in this state: "Do you desire to be wholly one; always day and night to be in one another's company? For if this is what you desire, I am ready to melt you into one and let you grow together, so that being two you shall become one, and while you live a common life as if you were a single man, and after your death in the world below still be one departed soul instead of two."' (192–3)

Joke or not, there was in such reflection a conception of the spiritual nature of humans that was to become important to reasoning on the nature of love in the centuries to follow. Aristotle understood the import of the doctrine that was implied, and he developed qualifications that were to be of enormous consequence, the more so surely since they accorded with common sense. To him friendship (at various phases of the discussion the relations of love and friendship were regarded interchangeably) is simply a sharing of interests between individuals of like disposition and character. In general Aquinas did not lose sight of the radical difference, remembering Aristotle's devastating criticism in the *Politics* (II, 1–1262b11): 'Aristotle quotes Aristophanes' remark that lovers long for the two of them to become one, but he points out that, seeing that if that happened, one or both would be destroyed, they in fact seek the kind of union which is appropriate to them: viz. to be together, to talk together, and to be united in other such relationships.' (*S.T.* Ia. 2ae. 28, 2) Once, however, in his early writings, when reflecting on the union of Father and Son 'in essentia', he spoke of love generally as 'having the faculty of uniting the loving and the loved.' (*Comment. In Sent. Petri Lombardi*, I, a.3)

In 'son attitude nuancée' Saint Thomas more than once remembered the words of Saint Paul that were so often used to support the Platonic reasoning on the lover's transformation—'I am crucified with Christ, nevertheless I live; yet not I, but Christ liveth in me.' (*Galatians*, II, 20). What was made of this had led to the formula of Saint Bernard that took on such authority that Thomas mistakenly credited it to Saint Augustine: 'Nor is our spirit more present where it lives than where it loves.' Thomas drove the metaphysical interpretation home: 'animam verius esse ubi amat, quia ibi est secundum nobilius esse, quod est secundum perfectionem ultimam.' (*Distinct*. XV. q.v.a. 3) This is, I think, the sense of—

Either was the others mine—

growth in perfection.

In his poems on the deaths of the Phoenix and Turtle Marston developed meanings that were quite unlike those of Shakespeare.

He wrote of the 'creature' that arose from the ashes of the two—immortality for them took the form of "issue". Identities were lost, in death the two became one with

> That wondrous rarenesse, in whose sweete
> All praise begins and endeth.

The Phoenix in Chester's poem had prayed—

> O holy, sacred and pure perfect fire. . . .
> Accept into your euer hallowed flame,
> Two bodies, from the which may spring one name.

For Chester, too, it seems, it is through the 'issue' that immortality is attained. Marston could also have had in mind 'the holy marriage' of the *Symposium* and the *Republic*, divine wisdom and virtue being engendered of the union of the soul with beauty. This would fit with the rest since he, like Seneca, was able to think of the eternal Ideas subsisting in the universal matter, or fire, that was God. But with or without contributions from Plato, in his conception the Phoenix and Turtle are lost in the anonymity of the foundation of all being.

In Shakespeare's poem there is no mention of an issue to the union—this had been 'married Chastitie'. The perfection of the union is insisted on—the two are joined as in one essence—yet it is the identities that survive. They had retained these in their ecstatic state, and, it seems, after death as well for they are then spoken of as 'Co-supremes and starres of love'. But the succession of paradoxes will not allow us to believe that there is the particular kind of separate existence for these two that Aristotle, and Aquinas most of the time, held to in refusing to take Aristophanes' myth as justified in metaphysics. Number may be slain, and yet the two remain distinct—this is neither the mersion into the 'boundlesse Ens' of Marston's stoicism, nor the persistent self-regard of Aristotle. The paradoxes construct another conception entirely that depends upon the character of infinity that the Neo-Platonists and Christians came to attribute to immaterial spirit. The idea had reached full expression in Plotinus:

'Let us consider once more how it is possible for an identity to extend over a universe. . . .'

'The light of our world can be allocated because it springs from a corporeal mass of known position, but conceive an immaterial entity, independent of body as being of earlier nature than all body, a nature firmly self-based or, better, without need of base: such a principle, incorporeal, autonomous, having no source for its rising, coming from no place, attached to no material mass, this cannot be allotted part here and part there: that would be to give it both a previous position and a present attachment. Finally, anything participating in such a principle can participate only as entirety with entirety; there can be no allotment and no partition. . . . Since, then, partition goes with place—each part occupying a place of its own—how can the placeless be parted? The unity must remain self-concentrated, immune from part, however much the multiple aspire or attain to contact with it. This means that any movement towards it is movement towards its entirety, and any participation attained is participation in its entirety. Its participants, then, link with it as with something unparticipated, something never appropriated: thus only can it remain intact within itself and within the multiples in which it is manifested.' (VI. 4. 7, 8 in MacKenna)

The discriminations became invaluable to Christians when reasoning on the Trinity but they were also important in reflecting upon the attachments of angels and humans. On the concept of *unio inconfusa* the words of the pseudo-Dionysius were centrally influential:

'And by the Beautiful all things are united together and the Beautiful is the beginning of all things, as being the Creative Cause which moves the world and holds all things in existence by their yearning for their own Beauty. And It is the Goal of all things, and their Beloved, as being their Final Cause (for 'tis the desire of the Beautiful that brings them all into existence), and It is their Exemplar from which they derive their definite limits; and hence the Beautiful is the same as the Good, inasmuch as all things, in all causation, desire the Beautiful and Good; nor is there anything in the world but hath a share in the Beautiful and Good. . . . This One Good and Beautiful is in Its oneness the Cause of all the many beautiful and good things. Hence comes the bare existence of all things, and hence their unions, their differentiations, their identities, their differences, their similarities, their dissimilarities, their communions of opposite things, the unconfused distinctions of their interpenetrating elements; the providences of the Superiors, the interdependence of the Co-ordinates, the responses of the Inferiors, the states of permanence wherein all keep their own identity.'[25]

So, in Shakespeare's poem, after the indication of a union in essence, that which follows explains how this could be—the persons having fled their bodies are freed from the confinements of quantity and space and time, what is possible for selves that are incorporeal and infinite. Number is slain, there is no division because there is no matter to be divided; distance extends infinitely and yet there is no such thing; hearts, souls, pass beyond the universe and still remain fixed; union is at once compound and simple.

Plato had not devised this way of reasoning. It took its rise among Stoics and Neo-Platonists, and was most perfectly articulated by Plotinus: '. . . he saw more clearly than any of his predecessors that separation and distinctness, as we usually conceive them, are essentially bound up with matter, space and time. Difference of essence in the immaterial world does not exclude, and in fact demands, co-presence and interpenetrability of the different entities, so that they can be at once really one and really different.'[26]

This provides the answers that will be given when answering the doubts implied in Thomas's questions: 'Is union one effect of love? Is mutual indwelling [*mutua inhaesio*] another? Is transport another?' (*S.T.* Ia. 2ae. 28, 1) But Aquinas, too, knows the same answer to his question, for even in referring again to Aristotle's reasoning in the *Ethics*, and repeating what he will always be remembering, that the appetite is imbued with the form of the object to which it is given, he nevertheless quotes Saint Paul: 'He

48

that is joined unto the Lord is one spirit.' (*I Corinthians*, VI, 17).

Saint Thomas will go on, 'It is through love that the Holy Spirit is in us, and that we possess it.' (*S.T.* I.a. 43, a.3). He and Ficino after him would be commenting on the same passage of the *Divine Names*: '[Love] means a faculty of unifying and conjoining and of producing a special commingling together in the Beautiful and Good: a faculty which pre-exists for the sake of the Beautiful and Good, and is diffused from this Origin and to this End, and holds together things of the same order by a mutual connection, and moves the highest to take thought for those below and fixes the inferior in a state which seeks the higher.' (IV. 12–709B).

Commenting on this same passage Ficino quotes Paul and repeats the formula, 'Amor impellit amantem in amatum se transferre.' (*Opera* [1576], II, 1067), and in his comment on the *Lysis* he not only goes beyond Plato, he is more particular than the pseudo-Dionysius: 'The end is this, that from two minds there is made one in will, from one will one life.' (*Opera* [1576], II, 1272).

In such ways the myth of the *Symposium* and the divine fury of the *Phaedrus* were taken into Christian thought. They were transmitted and enriched—by Saint Augustine, Hugues de Saint-Victor, Saint Bonaventura, Ficino may even have secularized them. They were at least 'tolerated' by Saint Thomas and Gerson. They took on a vibrant life in Saint John of the Cross and in *The Cloud of Unknowing*.[27] And something of the same life breathes in *The Phœnix and Turtle*.

III

The words in the poem that we have learned to recognize as bearing technical meanings relate the fantasy to ideas certain systems of thought develop in characterizing the nature and the effects of love. The poem proceeds in delineating the nature of changes in the nature of two persons that have come about through love and in death. It tells of the interchange of selves and their consuming. We are told that 'Division' grows together, and that what departs yet remains. 'Single Natures double name' may be merely another way of saying that the two are one, but in view of the rest it may signify that *natura naturans* and *natura naturata* are now one and the same, cause and effect swallowed up in timeless duration.[28]

As the strange assertions multiply we may think we detect a common character to the changes that are being told of, some likeness in the manner of them as well as in the results. Since we are told that what has taken place has followed from the devotion of the Phoenix and Turtle—'So they loved'—we suppose the key is in this, that through love a power has worked to join like to like and to reconcile the most radical oppositions in nature. At the very beginning it is said that two individuals through mutual love have become as one in essence. The rest seems to depend on that, but thereafter the particular union is characterized in surprisingly general terms—'Number' is obliterated, 'Propertie' is appalled, 'space' disappears. Taken together these seem to say that there is a way to thinking about human existence, when it takes a certain form, independently of quantity and dimension and time. Love not only has the power to enable us to conceive of life emancipated from such limits, for some it effects that very state, it effects a passage through death and it translates—these two have become

Co-supremes and starres of Love.

Since the technical terms, whether they are from theology or philosophy, belong particularly to speculation concerning spiritual matters, we are induced to consider the power at work as itself spiritual and divine. We are prepared for this also by being told that the love of the Phoenix and Turtle was 'married Chastitie'. Suggesting more the sympathy of spirits than of minds even, we may think of relationships we have heard of in the Arthurian stories, and of a spirituality some Christian and some Platonic philosophy would account for. There is in this even the possibility of the miraculous. But whatever the relationship, we know we are being apprised in this poem of a power Shakespeare often refers to elsewhere.

In *All's Well* Helena found herself subject to a power she could never deny however much it caused offense. She recognized it as love, but she also identified it with understanding. It promised the satisfaction that comes to those who are assured the universe itself is favoring them. Her words are at once pathetic and serene, and in their pathos they give us a feeling sense of what the fantastic funeral poem supplies through the paradoxes of philosophy and theology:

> What power is it which mounts my love so high?
> That makes me see, and cannot feed mine eye?
> The mightiest space in fortune nature brings
> To join like likes and kiss like native things.
> (I. i. 210–13)

She speaks of this power as "nature", yet it achieves effects quite beyond anything we could ascribe to that—a power beyond the reach of understanding. It leads to adoration—

> In his bright radiance and collateral light
> Must I be comforted, not in his sphere.
> (I. i. 84–5)

It is a power that makes use of nature for in uniting two it is re-uniting what in the beginning it created.

> If ever we are nature's these are ours. This thorn
> Doth to our rose of youth rightly belong;
> Our blood to us, this to our blood is born,
> It is the show and seal of nature's truth,
> Where love's strong passion is impressed in youth.
> (I. iii. 116–20)

There is still something else we see in the power working in the lives of the Phoenix and Turtle. It appears to be working as it were in a circulatory way partly in the sense Chapman had in mind when he referred to the golden chain of Homer and the *Theataetus*. He wrote of the 'essence' diffused in 'continuous succession' to all things. For him, rather differently than for Shakespeare, individuals, pursuing philosophy and honoring love, ascend to union with God—the emphasis is upon their reaching towards divinity. With Shakespeare the divine power raises the lovers to itself. Where the likeness lies is in the conception of a perpetual, circulatory activity.

Consumed in flames, the Phoenix and Turtle are said to have 'fled'. Their ashes remain on earth but they themselves have become stars, apparently at the threshold of Heaven, now sharing in the reign of the supreme power. As stars they are seen to be shining upon the very world they left, in which a dirge is being chanted and prayers are being offered for them. Serene, they confer serenity upon those praying.[29]

So much we may infer from the situation—a view of two realms seen at once, of a passage between them, of mourners looking up, of stars looking upon them. But the nature of the activity, of the transformations, of the elevations, is meanwhile being explained. 'Essence' signifies the inherent constitution of things through which perfection is accomplished and it refers as well to the grounds of all being. It is informed with a power that allows love to convert the lover into the beloved. It is through reference to it that we are able to conceive of the relations of persons freed from the limitations of space and time. We discern in this the reasoning of the Neo-Platonists and Scholastics, for whom the paradoxes of the poem are the coherences of reality. And in this circularity we are noticing that character to the divine love the pseudo-Dionysius handed on to Aquinas: that 'circulatio' proceeding from good to good, through eternity.[30] Much as in *All's Well*, the divine love works from above, through the native and the like, mounting on high those who love.

Reason had been taken aback in observing a sympathy so complete only a paradoxical not to say a mystical explanation was being offered to account for it. Acknowledging the truth, Reason was compelled to think Love would substantiate what nothing else could—

Love hath Reason, Reason none.

Yet it is Reason who found words to make the most extraordinary statement of all.

The lines—

> Beautie, Truth, and Raritie,
> Grace in all simplicitie—

introduce the Threnos. Until then the technical terms had stressed the condition of the union of spirits. Truth, beauty, love and constancy were named as abstractions, they were neither personified nor indicated as anything but attributes of the persons who were being honored. But here not only are these words identified with persons they are being named as embodied—

> Here enclosde, in cinders lie.

The words that appear for the first time are peculiarly important. 'Raritie', which certainly signifies 'rare excellence' (in any sense it is new at this time) may imply uniqueness. Marston uses the word similarly in this same volume:

> Let me stand numb'd with wonder, neuer came
> So strong amazement on astonish'd eie
> As this, this measureless pure Raritie.
> Lo now; th'xtracture of deuinest *Essence*,
> The Soul of heauens labour'd *Quintessence*.

'Simplicitie' is the time-honored word for God Himself, for purity and as the One.[31] 'Grace' we must take in all senses.

And so one might form this paraphrase—beauty and truth and all that is excellent, the grace that is God Himself, remains incorporate in the very ashes of those who have fled the bodies love has consumed.

The ashes remain, held in the urn the mourners see. If 'Grace in all simplicitie' is taken to mean divinity pure and whole, the presence of God, then in saying that He remains in the ashes the poem would be indicating the eventual resurrection of the body.[32]

The word 'in' points to this interpretation. The Anthem had emphasized, if nothing else, that in coming to an understanding of this union we must exclude from our thoughts any consideration of quantity and dimension. All indicated a condition only to be thought of as the interpenetration of infinite selves.[33] And now, in the burial of the ashes, when the theological meanings would have kept before us the doctrine that the body shared in divinity with the soul, the final paradox came forward, this time re-introducing the idea of dimension.

Scholastic as well as other reasoning would do the same: 'For God is in all things by His essence, power, and presence, according to His one common mode, as the cause existing in the effects which participate in His goodness. Above and beyond this common mode, however, there is one special mode belonging to the rational nature wherein God is said to be present as the object known is in the knower, and the beloved in the lover. And since the rational creature by its own operation of knowledge and love attains to God Himself, according to this special mode, God is said not only to exist in the rational creature, but also to dwell therein as in His own temple. So no other effect can be put down as the reason why the Divine Person is in the rational creature except sanctifying grace.' (*S.T.* I, 43, a.3).

IV

An analysis of the separable elements of the poem would never in itself establish the interpretation that here human love throws light upon the theology of the Trinity as that in turn does upon love. A number of writers have spoken of the poem as 'mystical', as embodying a 'vision', and if we should come to believe it deserves that character, we should probably be dependent on comparison with other works for confirmation.

We also need to take into account reasoning that points to essential features of the mystical state, and indeed we are obliged to do this in considering the conclusion of Professor Robert Ellrodt, that in *The Phœnix and Turtle* we are meeting with an idea 'perhaps more closely related to Christian mysticism than genuine Platonism.'[34] He does not go much beyond that, except in using the phrase 'unapprehended absolute', but if we ourselves wish to meet the question we have, for help, a useful exposition by Professor Paul Henry of the essential differences as well as like-

54

nesses in the two states: 'Two profound differences, perceptible even in their vocabulary . . . separate Christian from Plotinian mysticism: the doctrine of grace, with the cognate doctrine of prayer, and the doctrine of anguish and of the mystical "darkness".

'While Plotinus often describes the ecstasy in terms of "vision" and makes frequent use of the metaphor of light, especially to mark the immediacy of the vision and so to express once again the unity of the subject and the object of contemplation, his use of the terms "apparition" and "manifestation" is rare. . . . It would be possible to look in these two terms for an indication of the idea of grace and of self-giving on the part of the One, but the idea is utterly foreign to Plotinus' thought. . . .

'Plotinus sometimes speaks of prayer, and can even do so in a mystical context describing the relationship of the soul with the One; but, as the passage itself proves [V.1, 6, 9–11], "prayer" is a tension of the soul, the final leap in the dialectical process; it is not an appeal, not an expectation; it is neither the effect nor the occasion of a movement of grace or inclination on the part of God.

'In the passage of Augustine's *Confessions* which is most directly inspired by the *Enneads* and in which the parallelism of movement, ideas, and vocabulary is particularly close and constant, the words of Plotinus are: "Now call up all your confidence; you need a guide no longer; strain and see." And Augustine, quoting from the Psalm, writes: "I entered even into my inward self, Thou being my Guide, and able I was, for Thou wert become my Helper" (tr. Pusey). [VII. x. 16] In this inversion of a thought essential to Plotinus lies all the distance between Neo-platonic and Christian mysticism. . . .

'The absence of the notion of "darkness" is more significant still, because more unexpected. It seems to be called for by the logic of the system as another aspect of the negative theology, and it seems also to be presupposed by the very abundance of mystical imagery drawn from the field of light. Yet it is simply not there. The fact is that if for Plotinus the One is truly transcendent (and no one doubts that it is) the pagan philosopher did not know the specifically religious attitude of adoration; if some characteristics

of his God belong to the category of the *fascinosum*, more belong
to that of the *tremendum*. The One is within reach of the philosopher not so much because it is interior to man's mind as because
the union does not presuppose either the One's spontaneous
movement of love, grace, and mercy or man's consciousness of his
sinful and divided self.'[35]

The last line of Shakespeare's poem—

For these dead Birds, sigh a prayer—

appears to plead for favor. At the very first there had been suggestions of the awful and the profane; later, of the terrible. And when
we read of those enclosed, not in ashes, but in 'cinders', we may
sense something of the 'mystical darkness' Professor Henry spoke
of. Then, too, the tone of this prayer for the dead—here if anywhere in the poem is an echo of the 'complaint'—is quite in-
appropriate to Neo-Platonists, for whom, it has been well said,
salvation is an assured reward.

What else is there to go on? We recognize in the poem the out-
growth of profoundly moving experience. The lines are alive with
the conviction of the activity of a marvellous power. We notice
a certain stillness, as it were, in the state of the one writing who is
the witness to it. After the pitch of intonation and the incantatory
rhythm we are impressed by the peculiar bareness—statements
that do not permit exceptions, the absence of epithets, the lack of
particularity in the images, bodiless abstractions and bodiless
personifications. And yet nothing is vague. Putting all together we
may suppose this to be a strictly disciplined means of affirming
the sense of the very fullness of being through negation. A profound experience is being represented by anything but color and
music and passion.

The writing of the pseudo-Dionysius is, of course, not a poem
although in its fire and eloquence as well as in the energy of the
thought it is deeply stirring. And yet by comparison I think we
may make the point that if what he writes is to any degree a fair
representation of what is involved in the finest love, this is all that
it is, a characterization, not a representation. Yet by what is

striking in the comparison we may be led to accept the power of Shakespeare's poem as at least the residual impression of the experience the theologian is praising:

(The translator's somewhat florid style [C. E. Rolt] is yet admirable, and I would only observe that his use of the word 'yearning' to mean love was forced upon him in attempting to find a term to account for the rather strange preference of the pseudo-Dionysius for *eros* rather than for *agape*, which his Latin translators honored in using *amor* rather than *caritas* or even *dilectio*).

'[Yearning] means a faculty of unifying and conjoining and of producing a special commingling together in the Beautiful and Good. . . . And the Divine Yearning brings ecstasy, not allowing them that are touched thereby to belong unto themselves but only to the objects of their affection. . . . And hence the great Paul, constrained by the Divine Yearning, and having received a share in its ecstatic power says, with inspired utterance, "I live, and yet not I but Christ liveth in me"; true Sweetheart that he was and (as he says himself) being beside himself unto God, and not possessing his own life but possessing and loving the life of Him for Whom he yearned. And we must dare to affirm (for 'tis the truth) that the Creator of the Universe Himself, in His Beautiful and Good Yearning towards the Universe, is through the excessive yearning of His Goodness, transported outside of Himself in His providential activities towards all things that have being, and is touched by the sweet spell of Goodness, Love and Yearning, and so is drawn from His transcendent throne above all things, to swell within the heart of all things, through a super-essential and ecstatic power whereby He yet stays within Himself. . . . In short, both the Yearning and its Object belong to the Beautiful and the Good, and have therein their pre-existent roots and because of it exist and come into being.' (IV. 12–13 [712 A]).

The thought corresponds remarkably. But does this in fact offer insight into the difference? In *The Phœnix and Turtle* two are united, consumed, in a 'mutuall flame'. In the words of the pseudo-Dionysius just such a union is spoken of as 'a special commingling together in the Beautiful and Good'. In Shakespeare's poem the words 'Love' and 'Constancie' stand for the lovers. Possessed by love, these two, commingling, have come into another realm, having 'fled' their bodies. The pseudo-Dionysius may have been relating the angelic 'essences' to the Eternal Ideas. Shakespeare's words avoid such identification.

In *The Phœnix and Turtle* each lover enjoys unending satisfaction in which he remains himself. And though we may not find in the expression such passion as there is in Paul's cry that the pseudo-Dionysius is appealing to—'It is not I but Christ that liveth in me'—yet the words Shakespeare has chosen point to violence and dispossession:

>   the *Turtle* saw his right,
> Flaming in the *Phœnix* sight.

There is no cry here, only the shadow of one, but we sense the quietness of the statement and the tone as bought and paid for. In these two, beauty, truth, grace, existed to perfection, and in the assurance of that the words may succeed in communicating the conviction of peace.

Ficino, in recalling these same words of Paul speaking of love at work as 'uirtus quaedam unifica, & connectens, mirificèque commiscens, in ipso quod pulchro, bonoque propter pulchrorum, bonumque primo consistens' (*Opera* [1576], II, 1068). As he goes on, for all the eloquence, the piety, the care in which he makes evident his assimilation of orthodox teaching, he does not, I think, give the effect of the depth of the experience we get from Shakespeare's poem. Nor, for that matter, does any such power make itself felt in Bruno's '*furor*'. Poem after poem of his and Tansillo's tell of the fires of love and the consuming by fire, and when the question is asked, 'Why is love spoken of as fire?' the response points exactly to the sense of the figure in Shakespeare's poem: 'Because just as fire, being the most active of the elements, is able to convert everything, simple or compound, into itself, so love converts the beloved into the lover.'[36] I think the translation here does not do Bruno's eloquence much injustice: 'And just as by its essence the mind is in God who is its life, similarly by its intellectual operation and the operation of the will which follows upon that, the mind refers to its own light and its beatific object.' . . . 'Divinity cannot itself be the object before us, but only in similitude, and not such as is abstracted and acquired from the beauty and excellence of the body through the virtue of the senses but such as the mind can discern through the virtue of the intellect. When it has reached this state, the mind begins to lose the love and affection for every other sensible as well as intelligible object, for joined to that light it becomes that light and is made a very god.'[37]

It is much the same with Pico. There is again the same language, the transformation of the lover into the beloved, the consequent death and rebirth—'they are so perfectly united that each of them may be said to be two souls and both of them one only.' But again it seems that sensibility is being celebrated more than the power effecting the union, and there is certainly little to evoke the sense of the power of God. Even the sense of the beloved all but disappears in the representation of the ascent of the lover: 'Purged from Material dross and transformed into spiritual flame by this Divine Power, he mounts up to the Intelligible Heaven, and happily rests in his Father's bosom.'[38]

Or, to go back to the magnificent origin of much of this— Plotinus himself, wonderfully well in MacKenna's translation, does communicate something of the fire in his mind; 'knowing thus, in a deep conviction, whither he is going—into what a sublimity he penetrates—he must give himself forthwith to the inner and, radiant with the Divine Intellection (with which he is now one), be no longer the seer, but, as that place has made him, the seen.' (V. 8. 11). And as we follow this extraordinary intellection we notice, I think, a note of unclouded triumph such as we do not hear in Shakespeare's words. Whatever the satisfaction these communicate there persists in them the note of loss, and in the praise the tone of the plea. And so, if the ascription of the mystical is appropriate—and for my part I have come to the conclusion that it is—the Christian character as Professor Henry analyzed it is the more proximate.

When we turn to verse that we call mystical, I think we acknowledge the foremost quality to be a certain clarity. In the negative, there is no indication of tension, which I think signifies that all indication of desire or aspiration has been excluded. The note is of simple fulfilment. When Dante speaks of Beatrice—

> quella che imparadisa la mia mente—
> (*Paradiso*, xxviii, 3)

it is the very simplicity that extinguishes the possibility even of the metaphorical. In a more elaborately noted experience, again the air of factuality allows for no questioning: 'A thousand desires hotter than flame held mine eyes bound to the shining eyes, which remained ever fixed upon the grifon. As the sun in a mirror, not otherwise, the twofold beast was beaming within them, now with the attributes of one, now of the other.' (*Purgatorio*, xxxi, 118–23)

The particular conceit that allows for the development of the thought in Shakespeare's poem in Donne ends, as perhaps always with him, in the cross-play of satisfaction and anxiety. The intensity is focused more passionately than in Bruno, I think, but one would still less credit it as an expression of a mystical order even when the words point to such:

> The Phoenix ridle hath more wit
> By us, we two being one, are it.
> So, to one neutrall thing both sexes fit.
> Wee dye and rise the same, and prove
> Mysterious by this love.
> (*The Canonization*, 23–7)

Here, too, lover and loved have become one (and Donne may be making explicit use of Ficino)[39] but what the intellection has done here is the very opposite of what is spoken of as its function for true mystical experience, a function I think that may be ascribed to the complex reasoning in Shakespeare's poem: 'C'est souligner le paradoxe qui commande toute cette méthode: le Bien est au delà de l'intellectualité, et il est sa signification la plus intime. L'extase n'est pas une pensée, et elle est la source de toute valeur noétique.' 'Qui n's pas vécu l'immanence noétique n'est pas orienté vers la simplicité. Le spirituel qui n'a pas été décanté par l'intellectualité, le mystique qui n'a pas subi l'épreuve de la dialectique, reste toujours ambigu.' 'Si le mysticisme est *amour*, et s'il procure comme tel une unité supérieure à celle de l'intelligence, c'est à la condition que cet amour ait été épuré, authentifié par l'intelligence comme "amour spirituel". (*Enneads*, VI. 7. 35)'[40]

V

God shall be truly known, and those about her
From her shall read the perfect ways of honour
And by those claim their greatness, not by blood.
Nor shall this peace sleep with her; but as when
The bird of wonder dies, the maiden phœnix,
Her ashes new create another heir
As great in admiration as herself,
So shall she leave her blessedness to one
(When heaven shall call her from this cloud of darkness)
Who from the sacred ashes of her honour
Shall star-like rise as great in fame as she was,
And so stand fixed. (*Henry VIII*, V. v. 36–47)

From the beginning to its end the poem asks us to discover references to reality in the preposterous. Sub-human creatures mingle with abstractions, and we suppose there is meaning to the mingling. We sense also references to particular humans we are never quite able to certify in the names given legendary birds and in the celebration of virtues. When Reason speaks at the conclusion—which we are not so much induced to picture as an allegorical figure as to regard as our own inquiring at that very moment—we are met with a final contrast in which love is said to know more than Reason. Offering such support as experience can offer in interpreting the paradoxes we are left to accept what is never to be brought within the reach of thought.

We knew from the beginning—really in the mere sound of the

first words—we should be meeting with the mysterious and even with confusion, but as the poem went on this never tempered the almost unearthly lucidity that seemed always on the verge of breaking through. The confusion we first recognized when we learned some birds were being invited to the rite and others were excluded, for some of the reasons were hidden from us. Then, bare assertion imposed itself upon the outrageous, outfacing contradiction, in paradox after paradox, the language apparently simple but in fact occult. Yet the sense of the unexceptionable survived so assuredly, the suggestion of lucidity was so persistent, we could only think we were treating with truth.

A call to a requiem is followed by statements defining in abstract terms the state of the lovers in their sympathy and harmony. There then comes the concluding eulogy. But with the very last words the scene of the worship shifts, the congregation is enlarged to take in those attending to the re-enactment of the celebration. And now not only those invited to the mass but we ourselves, the readers, are instructed to pray. Yet the strangeness of it all and the impersonality persist, and in words that might have been expected to utter grief most openly, even to soliciting the participation of strangers, we are compelled to draw back—

For these dead *Birds*, sigh a prayer.

We know this is no mere breaking off, for although we as readers and also as ones included in the summoning, have had very little guidance on what to expect as the poem commenced: we had only been able to recognize the form it was taking as the parts were joined, but at the end we know enough to recognize that what had been undertaken was completed. The poem had commenced abruptly—and this would seem so even if Chester's introductory poem were still fresh in mind—for we were compelled to divine what occasioned this first injunction to a bird obscurely if at all identified—'the bird of lowdest lay.' We then followed along with the few uncertain directions while the burden of meaning grew. And then in the final lament, when the words were at once the most solemn and joyful, we found ourselves returned to the world in which we might be mourning our own friends.

The poem initially introduced us to a scene that was anything but familiar. We were asked, and were prepared, to imagine a hall—a meadow?—never described, where birds are gathering. Several are invited by name to come forward, others, also named, are forbidden to profane the place. The roles of the celebrants are indicated as ones they have been known to enact before. But the rite is never performed—all we have in fact is a summons leading us to anticipate the coming together of those who are invited, followed by an anthem and a lament.

Two individuals have died. There is awe and grief at their passing because they were who they were, and because their love was of a superlative kind. The nature of that love and its effects are explained—were it not that we learn this from what is called an anthem we would hardly know a liturgical rite was in process.

We see nothing happening until a hitherto unknown celebrant, Reason, enters to chant the dirge, and this gives us a deeper understanding of the purpose of the ceremony and of the marvel of the loves of these two. This accomplished, we are asked to pray, and with the words that we take to be addressed also to us, the readers, who are now for the first time acknowledged to be in the audience—we become privy to what the verses have been giving form to. We get to know this in some such way as a dreamer in awakening becomes privy to what he has been thinking in his dream, believing we perceive a method in the procession of images and thoughts in this vaguely indicated rite. We notice, too, as with many poems telling of dreams and visions, that the form is completed with the exhaustion of the questions the dream feeds on, not with the supplying of answers. The abruptness of the ending is in fact the sign the burden of the dream has been defined as, for example, we recognize in that abruptness with which Milton ended his poem—'I waked, she fled, and day brought back my night.'

Seeing how it was that our thoughts were led on we begin to understand that the hold the poem has had upon us is indeed of the kind we know in dreams and visions. And the more we credit the beauty and power in this re-creation of a fancy, the more we begin to think that the language treating of ideas of essence and participation and the eternal present harmonizes with the picturing of the preparations for a fantastic rite.

And now we find ourselves looking at the dream-like succession in still another way.

A dreamer is re-living a dream in which he himself is speaking. Two of his friends are dead and in the dream he seemed to be arranging their funeral rite. His friends had become birds and he was summoning other birds to the mass. In life his friends had embodied the perfection of love and constancy, and it seems there could have been no thought of their perishing. Because the legend of the phoenix is understood to tell something about the nature of love, and of immortality attained through sacrifice and resurrection, in the dream one of his friends appeared as a phoenix, the turtle as her mate, and their death through love became the means of entry into eternal life.

But the dream is wilder still, as if in the dreamer's thoughts there was a turbulence of equal strangenesses—not only humans become birds, and birds passing through fire into life, but such strangeness in attempting to hold on to what this referred to in actuality, ideas took such glory as eye could not hear, nor ear see. There were the drilled-in formulas of philosophers and churchmen, curiously distorted or expressed straightforwardly, that two may become one, that the heart has its reasons, that duration may be swallowed up in eternity, that nature in being born would also be nature perfected. All these strangenesses, these preposterous verities, seemed to be harmonious. For one matter was constantly impelling, the sense of the unimaginable, the reality of the sleep out of which all this was coming to birth. The preposterousness no more than the authentic particulars misrepresented the reality of that abyss. Reality was what might swallow up beauty and truth and constancy in the dark of the urn, obliterate all good, all that humans as much as the figures in the strange sequences of dreams were so curiously holding to. The preposterousness signified the possibility of endurance. And so, passing through the tragic scene, as thoughts succeeding each other in dreams, the two birds came into a place where there was company and light—the Supreme itself.

Most of the other poems in *Loves Martyr* embodied reflections on the passage from death into another life in largely philosophic expoundings. Chester's was the most elaborately imaginative, drawing upon a number of medieval poetic conventions—visions, the ascents into heaven, even the romantic epic. In using the symbol and legend of the phoenix Chester set the theme for the others to follow, and established the tone not only of the fanciful and mysterious but of the allegorical.

By its nature any such undertaking tempts ridicule. Private ritual, eulogy, particular philosophies risk seeming trivial by contrast with time-sanctioned funeral rites, and the glory of language equal to the faith of centuries. But the demand here as always was inescapable, the challenge was accepted, the risk taken, contempt defied.

Shakespeare's poem avoided every abuse. It is offered as a dream, and thereby, by definition, it escapes the most damaging pretentiousness. Such authority as dreams may claim to is shared with an at least equally mysterious image in one of the strangest of legends. Referring to the fantastic notion of a mass participated in by birds the dream calls attention to what it dare not call itself, a true rite. Developing the most intricate reasoning it insists upon limits to reason. By such means it honors what is barely if at all conceivable, leading through images and thought to the praise of what is beyond thought.

The dream takes off from one of those tricks of the mind in which the familiar takes on unfamiliar form, a group of mourners having become birds, even, possibly, the very poets preparing this volume becoming a swan and an eagle and a crow. The dead, of course, are legendary and miracle-working, birds who vanish into fire to take still other life. Those celebrating them as the Phoenix and Turtle themselves are bound to each other by duties and affections requiring fantastic observances in honor of happenings that outgo nature. For what has elicited the strange in the figuring has been the strangeness of the idea that two humans knew such concord they could be thought of as losing themselves in each other. And that in itself is so contrary to the nature of things that their merging must be thought of as the merging of spirits, departed from the world of time and space into measureless realms. And yet, by the very testimony of the regard for them as persons the mourners must continue to think of them as remaining themselves. It is the thought that love works such miracles, and that the universe is indeed such that it harbors them, that the dream took form in the preposterous images of winged creatures assembling for a sacrifice by fire; a strange person going by the name of Reason chanting a dirge; of an over-shadowing horror rejecting the profane. Which is as much as to say that what has brought the dream to birth, the burdens of loss and of hope and of faith, breaks through the preposterous figurings to authorize them.

The way was prepared in the strange manner of the anthem, the pairing of the opposites, the paradoxes defying sense as much as the conceit of the mass itself. The notion of the sympathy of the two had been immediately translated into an idea of two becoming one, and that idea led into one extension of speculation after another.

Because the legend allowed for the likening of love to fire, and since flame mingling with flame is perfect fusion, the sense forms of that which is also capable of perfect union, the truly incorporeal. That allows too for the fact of the ashes before which the rite is to take place, the union of bodies in which only the anonymous perishes, and identity survives.

And that in turn invites the strange balancing of familiar words—two and one, parting and remaining, remote yet not asunder, distance and no space. The result is not only the ampli-fication of all that seems fantastic, even impossible, for the images that commenced to take the form of birds assembling in an un-peopled place quickly dissolves, and at the end we are left with only the sense of the disembodied, where the words 'dead birds'

themselves only signify what are no longer even bodies, the formless ashes of humans. And so the dream ends in waking, in the
presence of the fact, in the request for a prayer to that which is not
even named, but which is dreamed to have transformed and
translated and deified persons.

NOTES

[1] *English Literature in the Sixteenth Century, Excluding Drama*, Oxford,
1954, p. 509.

[2] Kenneth Muir and Sean O'Loughlin, *The Voyage to Illyria*, London,
1937, pp. 128 and 134.

[3] *Shakespere and his Forerunners*, New York, 1902, I, 94.

[4] Marston was greatly attached to this way of valuing. In *Iacke Drums
Entertainment* (1601), for example, a young woman is being praised:

> Amazement, wonder, stiffe astonishment,
> Stare and stand gazing on this miracle,
> Perfection, of what e're a humane thought
> Can reach with his discoursive faculties.
> Thou whose sweet presence purifies my sense,
> And doest create a second soule in me. (Sig. H4v).

Astonishment, excellence, perfection—these are words that evidently relate
to firm beliefs. As Mr. P. J. Finkelpearl remarked, '[One] may see that this
language can be debased into a formula ... or that it can sound silly ...
But its recurrence in play after play suggests that [Marston] held an
unexamined hope or dream that unsullied purity and perfection still
existed or might exist in this fallen world.' (*John Marston of the Middle
Temple*, Cambridge, 1969, p. 241).

[5] It has been thought that here Seneca is all but anticipating Saint Anselm's
ontological argument for the existence of God.
   Professor Peter Dronke has remarked that Anselm's argument lies
behind the passage in *Loves Martyr* in which the Pelican contemplates the
sacrifice, and the same reasoning is at work in Cleopatra's praise of
Antony:

But, if there be or ever were one such,
It's past the size of dreaming. Nature wants stuff
To vie strange forms with fancy; yet, t'imagine
An Antony were nature's piece 'gainst fancy,
Condemning shadows quite. (*Antony and Cleopatra*,
V. ii. 96–100)

('*The Phœnix and the Turtle*,' *Orbis Litterarum*, XXIII [1968], 213.)

6 Philip Merlan, 'Greek Philosophy from Plato to Plotinus', in *The Cambridge History of Later Greek and Early Christian Philosophy*, 1967, p. 54.

7 The common Stoic doctrine was faithfully transmitted to the Renaissance: 'The soul of man is not formed from "Worldly Matter", but has its origin in the Heavenly Spirit of God. God, who is the Soul of the world, is also the source of man's soul, the life-principle which animates the body of man. God is even more; the Deity is said to be *in things* in such a sense that all animate entities are as parts of the Divine Essence.' (J. L. Saunders, *Justus Lipsius, The Philosophy of Renaissance Stoicism*, New York, 1955, p. 211).

At another place Marston wrote of the human mind as a spark of the divine fire—

our Intellectuall,
Compact of fire all celestiall,
Invisible, immortall and diuine.
(*The Scourge of Villanie*,
London, 1598, *Satyre* VIII).

The phrasing here is derived from the Stoic naming of God and Reason as 'the Primitive Fire'. Later Stoic doctrine was careful not to identify the infinite, individual self with the universal Mind, the part with the whole. Marston's phrase, 'All is *Mind*', may show the earlier inclination to pantheism.

8 This accords with a fixed belief of Chapman's: 'The desired union with God's goodness is to be attained through philosophy or learning together with contemplation, but all is futile without love.' (Ennis Rees, *The Tragedies of George Chapman, Renaissance Ethics in Action*, Cambridge, 1954, p. 22).

9 Plotinus is said to be the source of this passage, and citing it may serve to make clear how a number of notions in the poems in *Loves Martyr* derive from its substance. 'It is precisely because there is nothing within the

One that all things are from it: in order that Being may be brought about, the source must be no Being but Being's generator, in what is to be thought of as the primal act of generation.

... That station towards the One (the fact that something exists in presence of the One) establishes Being; that vision directed upon the One establishes the Intellectual-Principle; standing towards the One to the end of vision, it is simultaneously Intellectual-Principle and Being; and, attaining resemblance in virtue of this vision, it repeats the act of the One in pouring forth a vast power.

This second outflow is an image or representation of the Divine Intellect as the Divine Intellect represented its own prior, The One.

This active power sprung from essence (from the Intellectual-Principle considered as Being) is Soul.

Soul arises as the idea and act of the motionless Intellectual-Principle —which itself sprang from its own motionless prior—but the Soul's operation is not similarly motionless; its image is generated from its movement. It takes fullness by looking to its source; but it generates its image by adopting another, a downward, movement.

This Image of Soul is Sense and Nature, the vegetal principle. . . .

There exists, thus, a life, as it were, of huge extension, a total in which each several part differs from its next, all making a self-continuous whole under a law of discrimination by which the various forms of things arise with no effacement of any prior in its secondary.' (V. 2. 1–2—tr. MacKenna). (This has been identified as the source of Macrobius by Pierre Courcelle, *Les Lettres Grecques en Occident de Macrobe à Cassiodore*, Paris, 1948, p. 22).

[10] Professor Peter Dronke points out that Shakespeare's use of 'mine' here is cited by the O. E. D. as signifying 'an abundant source of supply'. ('*The Phœnix and the Turtle*', *Orbis Litterarum*, XXIII [1968], 217).

In describing the exchange of love Ficino also tells of a continuing increase: 'When you love me, you contemplate me, and as I love you, I find myself in your contemplation of me; I recover myself, lost in the first place by [my] own neglect of myself, in you, who preserve me. You do exactly the same in me. And then this, too, is remarkable: that after I have lost myself, if I recover myself through you, I have myself through you, and if I have myself through you, I have you sooner and to a greater degree than I have myself.' (*Commentary on Plato's Symposium, Oratio* II, *cap*. viii, tr. S. R. Jayne, Columbia, Missouri, 1944, p. 145).

The same sense is Pico's: 'Thus the Heart dyes in the flames of Intellectual Love, yet consumes not, but by the death "grows greater", receives a new and more sublime life.' (*A Platonick Discourse upon Love*, tr. Thomas Stanley, ed. E. G. Gardner, Boston, 1914, p. 70 [III, iv]).

[11] Jean Trouillard, *L'Un et l'Ame selon Proclos*, Paris, 1972, pp. 10–11.

[12] *Saint Bernard on the Love of God*, tr. and ed. T. L. Connolly, Westminster, Maryland, 1937, p. 190.

In this matter it seems that Christian mysticism accords with some other dispositions. Bruno, for example, is very probably keeping close to Plotinus: 'The heroic spirit, he says in the first dialogue of the second part [of the *Eroici Furori* (ed. P. H. Michel, Paris, 1954, p. 308)], will ever aspire to more excellent and magnificent objects "until he sees himself elevated to the desire of divine beauty in itself, without similitude, figure, image, and species, if it be possible; and more, if he knows how to accomplish such." The impetus of the philosopher's love may indeed carry him beyond the knowledge of the ideas to a union—in exaltation if not in knowledge—with the Plotinian superessential entity which is the source of ideas and all that is ontologically subsequent to them.' (J. C. Nelson, *Renaissance Theory of Love, The Context of Giordano Bruno's Eroici Furori*, New York, 1958, p. 189).

Mr. A. Alvarez' analysis of Shakespeare's language in this poem may serve to corroborate my application of the observation of Saint Bernard: 'As the purity of the love echoes through the purified language, so the poem too, section by section, refines and withdraws itself. The structure is precise and coherent: the invocation gives the setting and announces the theme; in the anthem is the descriptive argumentation; the bare statements of the Threnos are the climax and conclusion. The topics of the poem stretch out towards abstraction, from the "chaste wings", through the abstract concepts of the world of Reason, to the transcendentals of the world of Love.' ('William Shakespeare: *The Phœnix and the Turtle*', in *Interpretations*, ed. John Wain, 2nd ed., London, 1972, pp. 5–6).

[13] Winthrop Wetherbee, *Platonism and Poetry in the Twelfth Century*, Princeton, 1972, p. 205.

In writing most valuably of what Shakespeare's poem owes to the central pattern of the 'complaints of nature' Professor Dronke is led to the conclusion that Reason 'at the very moment of *ascending* into divine Love, *descends* into the world to act as Chorus, to participate in the love-death of two birds.' Similarly, 'the two birds, precisely by departing from the world, become its *angeloi*; the lovers, by living towards the fulfilment of their love in death, provide a "patterne of love" for the world they leave behind. So too, in the Chartrain poets, Natura's quest for a pattern of perfection in Heaven succeeds in bringing fertility to the earth. So too in Chaucer's *Parlement of Fowles* Scipio's way of askêsis brings forth the love-dream of Venus and ends in Natura's fullness and *comune profite*. So too, in Ficino's and Pico's mythography of the Graces, Castitas and

Voluptas are completed by Pulchritudo—the end of the ascent is not in the rapture, but in the fructifying return to the world.' ('*The Phœnix and the Turtle*', *Orbis Litterarum*, XXIII (1968), p. 219).

The issue that arises does not concern specific obligations on Shakespeare's part to Alain's or Chaucer's poems, or to others, but to the 'pattern'. This is to say, an action in which persons or powers dwelling on earth ascend to an upper realm with a petition to deities. The petition granted, divine favor is returned in some form to the creatures on earth. In this convention the figures may be mythical or fanciful beings or abstract powers, and these together with the activities are to be referred to the conditions set by Platonic philosophies. It is said, for example, that the principle sources of Alain's thought are in the pseudo-Dionysius and Boethius. (G. Raynaud de Lage, *Alain de Lille, Poète du XIIe Siècle*, Montreal, 1951, p. 68).

As I see it, the plan of *The Phœnix and Turtle* is to be compared to that of Alain's poem in only two features—each poem treats of two realms and passage between them, and each gives a remarkable significance to the narrator. But these are features common to other conventions, and I see nothing in Shakespeare's poem of that most characteristic element (that Chester makes so much of), an ascent into a celestial realm where a petitioner makes a plea, where there are extended debates, and a determination or a verdict is supplied before there is a return to the lower realm. Professor Dronke, however, sees this 'pattern' in the role of Reason: 'Reason transcends herself if the love that is *parting* from the world can still be kindled, can still *remain*, in those who watch and participate. Thus the divine faculty of Reason, at the very moment of *ascending* into divine Love, *descends* into the world, to act as Chorus, to participate in the love-death of two birds.' (p. 219).

I can see that what Professor Dronke says explains how it is that Reason can at one moment interpret what at another moment confounds it, and that this would require its functioning differently in the two realms. But even to confirm this I think one ought to be able to point to some indication that it is Reason who ascends and descends, and I do not find this.

I find a similar inconclusiveness in another of Professor Dronke's suggestions, that the death of the birds is paralleled by 'Reason's dying into love. A neoplatonist might think of a further parallel: Anima Mundi is resolved into Ratio, and both are resolved into the "boundlesse Ens". A theologian could see a parallel in the Trinity, with Son and Spirit, Phoenix and Dove, dying eternally into the Father.' (p. 219) These suggestions, too, as Professor Dronke sees it, would follow in line with the matter of the complaint of nature. But if, as I believe, the influence of that pattern is relatively slight it is unwise to introduce such conceptions as that of the

Anima Mundi or 'the boundlesse Ens' and some others without examining the language of the poem as carefully as Professor Cunningham did in establishing its coherence with Scholastic usage. It is in taking account of such an analysis, I think, that one may control better the ramifications of Shakespeare's meanings. (See below, note 16).

Professor Dronke has performed a wonderful service in illustrating the wealth of tradition that supports Shakespeare's conception. Although I do not believe his interpretations support his most important conclusion, I believe that conclusion to be substantially right. 'I cannot agree with the most recent critic, Robert Ellrodt ['An Anatomy of *The Phœnix and the Turtle*', *Shakespeare Survey*, 15, Cambridge, 1962, p.99] that "the tone is throughout funereal". I find the tone exhilirating—and at the same time serene. The exhiliration, one might say, belongs to the drama in which the birds participate, the serenity to the unmoved exemplars that make the moving participation possible. . . . There is something rarefied about it, yet it remains in touch with human qualities, with the meaning of "true" and "fair" in the world; while it tells of birds and the perfection of love, it tells something relevant to imperfect human love.' (p. 220).

14 It is not necessary here to follow the entire argument of Professor Peter Dronke that 'the bird of lowdest lay', the Phoenix herself, while still alive is summoning mourners to the funeral. ('*The Phœnix and the Turtle*', *Orbis Litterarum*, XXII [1968], 208–209). The introductory 'Let' should be emphasized, I think—it is the arranger of the rite who allows the legendary bird as the symbol for the regenerative powers of love to watch over an imagined service for two who have indeed died. Being the symbol it is, the bird is known to participate in past, present and future as a timeless instant. Observing a sacrifice and a funeral the bird is participating in a phase of its continuing life. The arranger of the rite, or rather, the one reporting its preparations and the process, is free to conceive of the symbol in two forms simultaneously—as the eternal principle and as the form it has taken in one of the humans who has died.

The idea of the eternal present is also being exploited later, I believe, when the souls of the Phoenix and Turtle, inhabiting stars, are represented as shining upon those attending the funeral rite. (See below, note 29).

15 'Shakespeare's Theology', *A Review of English Literature*, V (October 1964), 82.

16 The succession of abstract words—Beautie, Truth, Love, Constancie—signify absolute perfection, and others that bring with them specialized references from philosophy and theology reinforce that meaning and give

it a special cast. As they do a question forms—is the poem celebrating human or divine love? There are many discriminations to make and in the end the answer will depend more upon our sense of the substance of the poem as a whole than upon what we make of the use of a group of particular words. I believe Professor Merchant has it right when he says that in this poem, Shakespeare makes 'the matters of Trinitarian theology and human love mutually illuminating'. ('Shakespeare's Theology', *A Review of English Literature*, V [October, 1964], 79).

Much will depend upon what we make of the use of the word 'essence', and in a remarkable study Professor J. V. Cunningham showed its crucial importance. ('"Essence" and *The Phœnix and Turtle*', *Journal of English Literary History*, XIX [1952], 265–76). We shall need to retrace his steps.

> So they loved as love in twaine,
> Had the essence but in one.

In *The Two Gentlemen of Verona* Valentine said of Silvia, 'She is my essence' (III. i. 182), and Professor Cunningham refers to this in signifying what is meant by 'the identity of essence' (p. 268) in *The Phœnix and Turtle*. His argument is so closely knit he should be quoted fully: 'The relation of the Phoenix to the Turtle is now clear. It is conceived and expressed in terms of the scholastic doctrine of the Trinity, which forms in this sense the principle of order of the poem. The Phoenix and Turtle are distinct persons, yet one in love, on the analogy of the Father and the Son in the Holy Ghost.' (p. 276).

Professor Cunningham is re-inforced in this conclusion on the one hand by his belief that union in love as understood by the Neo-Platonists did not allow for a survival of identity: 'It is not unlike, of course, the Neo-Platonic union, in which the soul, being reduced to the trace of the One which constitutes its resemblance to it, is absorbed, submerged, and lost in the presence of the One. There is no more distance, no doubleness, the two fuse in one.

'But the language here is Latin and has passed, as had the doctrine of Plotinus, through the disputations of the Schoolmen: *essence, distincts, division, property, single nature's double name, simple, compounded*. Furthermore, the chief point of Shakespeare's poem is lost in the Plotinan formulation: for the central part of the poem consists wholly in the reiteration— line after line as if the poet would have you understand even to exhaustion —of the paradox that though identical the two are distinct; they are both truly one and truly two. Thus, for example, in the Plotinan union there is no interval between the two—*And no space was seen*—but the contrary element of the paradox—*distance*—is lacking.' (p. 270). And on the other, his conclusions are sustained by the conviction that 'the doctrine of the poem is not sanctioned by the scholastic doctrine of human love'. (p. 273)

73

Professor Cunningham observes that for Saint Thomas and scholastic-ism generally it is possible to say only of the members of the Trinity that different persons are one in essence—'the absolute reality of God's nature [*rem absolutam quae est essentia*], where there is sheer unity and simplicity.' (*S.T.* Ia. 28, 4; *sicut una et eadem est essentia trivium personarum—De Potentia* Q. II. a. v.).

The use of the word *essence* with respect to the Trinity is not, of course, confined to scholastic writing. Professor Dronke, for one, refers to the *Praefatio* to the Trinity in the Roman liturgy: 'sine differentia discretionis ... in personis proprietas et in essentia unitas.' ('*The Phœnix and the Turtle*', *Orbis Litterarum*, XXIII [1968], 214).

Neither humans nor angels may be said to participate in union of that nature although there are other unions in which *essence* is shared. The reasoning goes in this way: The essence of the human soul is its intellec-tive power. In functioning it takes to itself what it knows, which is itself essence, and it thereby increases in perfection, for essence is related to being as potency to act. 'The proper object of the human intellect is ... the intelligible essence whose concept it abstracts from the data of sense experience. The *essences* of things, as definable by their *quiddities*, are the objects that our human intellect is eminently fitted to know.' (Etienne Gilson, *Elements of Christian Philosophy*, New York, 1960, p. 227).

This union of the knower and the known reaches its completion for Saint Thomas only if knowledge is comprehended in love. 'In the Divine Persons God is said to be as that which is known in him who knows, or as the loved is in the lover; for the creature itself attains to God by knowing and loving Him through the Divine Operation.' (*S. T.* I, 43, 3). 'Love is a more powerful unifying force than is knowledge.' (*S. T.* Ia. 2ae. 28, 1).

It follows that the union of souls in love is the actualizing of the essence of God through love. That union is the sharing of virtue and wis-dom. 'For just as by his intellectual power man participates in the divine knowledge through the virtue of faith, and in the divine love through the virtue of charity in his power of will, so too through the nature of the soul he participates, by way of a kind of likeness, in the divine nature, in con-sequence of a certain rebirth or recreation.' (*S. T.* Ia 2ae. 110, 4). 'And therefore Augustine says the soul is more truly where it loves than where it lives because it is there according to its more noble being, which is in accord with ultimate perfection.' (*Comment. Petri Lombardi*, Liber I, Sent. Dist. XV. q.5 a.3).

Pursuing such reasoning, Pierre Rousselot showed how in Thomas one may speak of a sharing of essence by humans:

'L'amour ne donne donc pas l'aimé à l'amant en lui communiquant comme un *autre* exemplaire de la même essence (ce qui est le cas des intellections *per speciem*), ni en lui communiquant l'essence réelle elle-même dans sa totalité (ce qui est le cas de l'intellection *per essentiam*), mais en le soumettant au principe de vie de l'être aimé, en lui ôtant son individualité *privée* pour le constituer partie d'un tout nouveau. Et si l'on peut encore ici parler de *ressemblance*, c'est "secundum quod potentia habet similitudinem ad actum ipsum" (1 a 2 ae q. 27 a.3): il ne s'agit pas en effet de ressemblance entre deux égaux, et, plus l'amour est amour, plus l'aimant est totalement subordonné à l'aimé et informé par lui.

'La doctrine de l'*amatum in amante* trouve une application théologique dans la théorie thomiste de la grâce (1 q. 8 a. 3 ad 4—1. q. 43 a. 3—4 CG 23.9). "C'est par l'amour qu'il cause en nous que le Saint Esprit est en nous, et que nous le possedons." La grâce, ce principe de nature divine, est tout entière *tendance*, mouvement vers la gloire.' (*Pour l'Histoire du Problème de l'Amour au Moyen Age*, Münster, 1908, pp. 84-5, n. 8. [*Beiträge sur Geschichte der Mittelalters*, Band VI. Heft 1]).

Moreover, Shakespeare's use of the word *had* seems to be warranted in this light:

'S. Thomas nie que l'amour opère formellement la possession réelle. "Coniungere secundum rem non est de ratione caritatis, et ideo potest esse habiti et non habiti" (Car. a.2 and 6—cp. de Spe a. 1 ad 11, et les articles où il traite des éléments constitutifs de la béatitude). *Posséder*, *tenir*, c'est, d'après lui, le partage des facultés *appréhensives* dont la principale est l'intelligence: c'est par conséquent l'intelligence dont l'opération nous béatifera en nous rendant possesseurs de l'Essence divine.' (p. 84).

Saint Thomas does not consistently allow for such a union as the pseudo-Dionysius conceives of, union in ecstasy, and he often emphasizes the sense of self-regard that Aristotle insisted on, yet there is reason to believe that in his different emphases there did persist a notion of a union probably best thought of as mystical:

'. . . c'est par son *esse* que la personne est unique et incommunicable. Par suite, son incommunicabilité n'est pas fermeture, ni son unité un isolement radical, au sens où Kierkegaard écrit "qu'il n'y a pas de rapport direct entre sujet et sujet", sous pretexte que "chaque homme particulier est seul." Du point de vue thomiste, l'incommunicable singularité de la personne humaine n'est pas une limitation purement négative, parce que l'être contracté en ses déterminations et qui fait sa plénitude intérieure, est ce par quoi chacun est relié à tous les autres. "Une communauté transcendentale, écrit le P. de Finance, pénètre ma personnalité dans des profondeurs. Et je dois ma réalité la plus incommunicable à cette communion." *Etre et Agir*, p. 114.' (Joseph Rassam, *La Métaphysique de Saint Thomas*, Paris, 1968, p. 121. See also p. 127).

'In Ia. 77, I St. Thomas points out that in God alone are being and doing one and the same; in all creatures there is a real distinction between essence and powers. The theological interest of his use of the distinction here is that it establishes an "ontological" rather than a "personalist" perspective for grace. Grace is prior to its "personal" expression in action. . . . One may perhaps detect mystical implications in St. Thomas's *essentia* and find in it a notion not unlike Meister Eckhart's *Grund* of the soul.' (Cornelius Ernst, *Summa Theologia*, XXX, Blackfriars, 1971, pp. 122–3).

(Professor Cunningham's conclusion was made possible in part by his exclusive attention to the Anthem—Professor R. G. Underwood pointed out that the Threnos played no part in his interpretation. *Shakespeare's 'The Phœnix and the Turtle': A Survey of Scholarship*, Salzburg, 1974, p. 220]. All Students of Shakespeare's poem must be deeply grateful for Professor Underwood's careful analyses.)

If so much is allowed, then it seems Shakespeare's words could be accommodated to 'the scholastic doctrine of human love'. But that this should lead ineluctably to an interpretation of the poem itself as Christian does not follow—the illumination of Trinitarian theology that Professor Merchant spoke of will need to be certified by other considerations than those turning on the conception of the sharing of essence. In this respect a glance at the reasoning and language of Leone Ebreo is particularly informative. Much that he writes seems conventionally Neo-Platonic, and at the same time the debts to scholasticism are as evident. But where Ficino, for example, would ordinarily take care to remain close to Christian orthodoxy, Leone took as great care at the crucial points to depart from it. While the language and reasoning in Shakespeare's poem would not, I believe, allow for the use of Leone as a sufficient gloss, I believe one should, nevertheless, notice the words of the *Dialoghi d'Amore* if only to see how closely they correspond to Shakespeare's sense in this matter.

'It is not meet, Sophia, to speak of the intrinsic love of God, as lover and beloved, with the same tongue and lips with which we are wont to speak of earthly loves. The co-existence of lover and beloved creates no diversity in Him, but rather it is this intrinsic relation which makes His unity more perfect and more truly one; because His divine essence [*la sua divina essenzia*] would not represent the highest form of life did it not reflect in itself the beauty and wisdom of the beloved, the wise lover, and the perfect love of them both. And as in God the knower, the thing known and the act of knowing are all one and the same, although we say that the knower is made more perfect by increase of knowledge and that both he and the object known are necessary to cognition; so also in God the lover, the beloved and their love are all one and the same, and although we count them to be three and say that the lover is informed by the beloved and that love derives from them both (as from the father and mother), yet

76

the whole is one simple unity and essence [*una simplicissima unità ed essenzia*] or nature, which can in no way be divided or multiplied.' (*The Philosophy of Love*, tr. F. Friedeberg-Seeley and Jean H. Barnes, London, 1937, p. 299–bk. 3).

'Man is intelligent and the nature of fire is a thing which he understands. Now when man and fire are in potentiality with respect to understanding they are two separate things, and the intellection, also in potentiality, makes a third; but when the human intellect actively apprehends fire it unites with its essence [*si unisce con l'essenzia del fuoco*] and is one with fire in the mind, and so too this same intellection, when active, is the same as the intellect and the intellectual fire, and they are no longer divided. In the same way the potential lover is other than the potential beloved and they are two persons, while potential love makes a third which exists neither in the beloved nor in the lover; but when the potential lover becomes actual he is made one and the same with the beloved and with love. If, then, you can see how these three different natures may become one and the same in actuality, how much greater will be their union in supreme and divine actuality where they form one pure and single nature without division of any kind.' (pp. 303–4).

17 'The Phoenix and Turtle', *Englische Studien*, XXXIII (1904), 337–84.

18 *Essays and Addresses*, London, 1929, 166–8.

19 See, for example, the reasoning in *Summa Contra Gentiles*, II. c. 79.

20 Erigena writes that as air loses its substance when transformed by the light of the sun, iron and other metals are made liquid by fire and become fire, so 'the bodily substance passes over into the soul, not that it may perish but that it may be preserved in a finer essence'. (*De divisione naturae*, V. 8).

21 The paradoxes in the poem quite uniformly assert that while two persons are intrinsically different and physically separate they are also ever-present to each other. The contradictory is never lost sight of, and as a result the difficulty of maintaining the claims of philosophy or theology to resolve the contradiction is never removed. The Stoic solution—as in Marston's 'All is *Mind*'—would be inapplicable here since in reducing all to matter, even to fire, identity is lost, and what has occasioned the initiating claim, the hope or belief that love confers immortality upon lovers, would be fatally disappointed.

However inadequate the argument as it was made by Plato that love would result in everlasting union, the Neo-Platonists with the help of a certain contribution from Stoicism devised a system that would sustain the claim, and that would be invaluable to Christians. From the Stoics there developed the means of considering the soul or the self to be infinite. The Neo-Platonists discovered how to develop a conception in which the immaterial self, now conceived of as infinite, would allow for just such perfect commingling. Christians would develop the reasoning still further when they demonstrated how an infinite, immaterial soul could inform a body.

Shakespeare's paradoxes require us to conceive of persons as not confined within the dimensions of space or time. They also require us to conceive of the undying existence of such beings—or perhaps essences. What is said in the poem fits these conceptions of *unio inconfusa* and *inlocalitas* as the theologians had worked them out. What is said in the poem also precludes the idea that the realm of being in which the immortals live is 'the boundlesse Ens' of the Stoics. Seneca says that after the general conflagration 'the souls of the blest . . . shall be changed again into our former elements'. (To Marcia, XXVI. 6). They will return 'to the place from which they came . . . the celestial realms of thought' (*Ep.* LXXIX. 12). With such ideas Marston's line, 'Ought into nought can never remigrate' might be a rebuttal of the doctrine he understood Shakespeare's poem to express, whether that were Platonist or Christian.

Plotinus developed an idea of 'the infinite self': 'Extension is of body; what is not of body, but of the opposed order, must be kept free of extension; but where there is no extension there is no spatial distinction, nothing of the here and there which would end its freedom of presence.' (VI. 4. 8).

'At this point in Plotinus' thought we are obviously very far indeed from the vitalist corporealism of the Stoics. His real universe of interprenetating minds is not simply the organic universe of Posidonius transposed to a higher level of being. It is a highly original conception based on ideas derived from Plato and Aristotle. We can see well here one of the most important and interesting characteristics of Plotinus' thought, the way in which he saw more clearly than any of his predecessors that separation and distinctness, as we usually conceive them, are essentially bound up with matter, space and time. [VI 4 (22) 4]. Difference of essence in the immaterial world does not exclude, and in fact demands, copresence and interpenetrability of the different entities, so that they can be at once really one and really different.' (A. H. Armstrong, 'Plotinus', in *The Cambridge History of Later Greek and Early Medieval Philosophy*, 1967, p. 248.) (For what has been concluded concerning the origin of these discriminations see J. M. Rist, 'The Problem of "Otherness" in the *Enneads*', *Le Neoplatonisme: Colloques Internationaux du Centre National de la Recherche Scientifique*, Paris, 1971, p. 80).

As the conception was taken up by Neo-Platonists and Christians, and it became one treating the relation of the divine to all else, of soul to body, of the infinite to the finite, in Porphyry, Augustine, Proclus, in so many, the idea of the *unio inconfusa* made use of analogies—the minglings of liquids, most especially of water and wine, of air and light, and of flames. To summarize briefly: 'Entre la juxtaposition et le mélange proprement dit il y a place pour une union d'un type nouveau, à savoir, une union sans confusion . . . qui laisse subsister chacune des substances dans son intégrité. C'est l'union au sens plein du mot, sort d'intermédiaire entre les deux autres, qui a en commun avec la κρᾶσις de rapprocher intimement les deux substances au point d'un faire un seul être, mais qui, comme la παράθεσις, n'implique pas leur anéantissement. C'est ce qui permit à Plotin d'affirmer sans se contredire que le "nous" désigne tantôt l'âme seule, tantôt le composé. Tout en laissant à l'âme sa primauté et en définissant par elle "l'homme véritable", il reconnait lui-même que "l'animal" ou ce qu'il appelle encore "la substance totale de l'homme" est un mélange d'éléments supérieurs et inférieurs étroitement unis de telle sorte qui lorsque le corps souffre, nous pouvons dire que c'est nous qui souffre.

'Ce mode d'union original est le propre précisément des substances spirituelles, soit qu'elles s'unissent entre elles, soit qu'elles se joignent aux corps. Pour le comprendre, il faut faire abstraction de ce que nous révèlent les sens, mais il n'est pas tout à fait sans analogie dans le domaine des corps, comme le montre l'exemple de la lumière et de l'air, qui s'unissent sans se corrompre. C'est pourquoi le terme l'illumination est particulièrement apte à désigner cette présence de l'âme au corps. Ne voyons pas en elle uniquement une réalité d'ordre gnoséologique. Nous la retrouvons dans des contextes qui en eux-mêmes n'ont rien à voir avec le problème de la connaissance. Cependant, comme cette action de l'âme a pour effet d'imprimer son reflet dans les corps et de rendre ainsi la matière intelligible à des degrés divers, elle n'est pas non plus sans rapport avec l'illumination intellectuelle.' (E. L. Fortin, *Christianisme et Culture Philosophique au Cinquième Siècle*, Paris, 1959, pp. 118–19).

Letter 137 of Saint Augustine depends on such reasoning, and of course this is drawn on in speaking of the Incarnation.

One needs to understand how Platonists allow for the retention of identity in such unions. There is of course a current of thought in which the identity is lost, and it is in thinking of this that Professor Cunningham felt he must exclude a Plotinian interpretation of Shakespeare's poem. ('"Essence" and *The Phœnix and the Turtle*', *Journal of English Literary History*, XIX [1952], 270). But Plotinus insists on the paradox of plurality in unity: 'Soul was one and many; the many souls fore-existed in the All not potentially but each effectively; that one collective Soul is no bar to the variety; the variety does not abrogate the unity; the souls are apart without partition, present each to all as never having been set in opposition; they are no more hedged off by boundaries than are the multiple items of knowledge in one mind; the one Soul so exists as to include all souls; the nature of such a principle must be utterly free of boundary.' (VI. 4. 4). And even in the union with the One, it seems, it is possible to think of the self surviving: 'The self, we may say, is totally *one with the One*, but as a subject, as *itself*.' (G. J. P. O'Daly, *Plotinus' Philosophy of the Self*, Shannon, 1973, p. 85).

Aquinas, too, takes up with this reasoning, and commenting at one place on the pseudo-Dionysius when he is writing of the unions of Angels —*unitiones Angelorum*—in intellection and in affection, he said: 'Such union does not take away the distinction that is the property of each' and what remains are *inconfusae discretiones*. (*In Librum Beati Dionysii De Divinis Nominibus Expositio*, ed. Ceslai Pera, Turin, 1950, p. 89–#283).

If now we return to what is meant by

And had the essence but in one,

and take that to signify an essential union of a particular order, that the souls of the two are thereby increasing forever in perfection, then this would require for understanding precisely what the paradoxes stress— these two are to be regarded as free from the limits of dimension, quantity, and time.

[22] 'Yes, love, for the soul abides no less in what it loves than in what it animates; unless perhaps unwilling necessity is considered to be a stronger bond than free and ardent choice.' (*De Praecepto et Dispensatione*, XX, 60). In this whole matter of the Christian use of the ancient, and particularly Platonic teaching on love and friendship I am greatly indebted to Jean Orcibal, 'Une Formule de l'Amour Extatique de Platon à Saint Jean de la Croix at au Cardinal de Bérulle', *Mélanges Offerts à Étienne Gilson*, Paris, 1959, pp. 447–54).

[23] N. J. Perella, *The Kiss, Sacred and Profane*, Berkeley, 1969, p. 96; *Bernart de Ventadorn, Seine Lieder*, ed. Carl Appel, Halle, 1915, p. 227.

The conceit of the exchange of hearts was commonly used in medieval Arabic poetry and thereafter in the Provençal poets. Some expressions had it that hearts changed places in the lovers' bodies, in some the words were only to be taken symbolically. An important consideration often was that love was said to be between equals and not in the submission of one to the other. In the vast range of troubadour poetry there were, of course, traces of spirituality and even reasoning about the relations of human and divine love. Later, as in the complaints of nature, there will be some evident use of Platonism. It is well said that Dante and Petrarch in their most complex reasoning using such a figure as that of 'the eaten heart' put the concrete language of this convention to the use of ideas concerning the union of souls. (René Nelli, *L'Érotique des Troubadours*, Toulouse, 1963, p. 215).

24 Codice Trivulziano, in *Scritti letterari*, ed. Augusto Marinoni, Milan, 1974, p. 67.

25 Dionysius the Areopagite, *On the Divine Names and the Mystical Theology*, tr. C. E. Rolt, London, 1920 [IV, 7–704A–C].

26 A. H. Armstrong, 'Plotinus', in *The Cambridge History of Late Greek and Early Medieval Philosophy*, 1967, p. 248.
Porphyry said that while he was away on a journey his intelligible self remained with his wife. (*Ad Marcellam*, 280; Nauck 22).

27 Jean Orcibal, 'Une Formule de l'Amour Extatique', *Mélanges Offerts às Étienne Gilson*, Paris, 1959, p. 403.

28 This is a suggestion of Peter Dronke, 'The Phoenix and the Turtle', *Orbis Litterarum*, XXIII (1968), 218. Bruno's *De la Causa* develops this conception into a comprehensive theory.

29 The namings in this line give us little to go on in deriving an idea of the system to which this indication of the translation of souls or persons belongs. Professor Dronke does extremely well in suggesting possibilities through questions: 'Is it not precisely because Phoenix and Turtle have ascended to heaven in their mutual flame, because the attributes truth and beauty have thereby attained eternity and been united at their source, that they can for ever be participated in by the other birds, and leave their signature in the created world?' ('The Phoenix and the Turtle', *Orbis Litterarum*, XXIII [1968], 211). He finds a possible illustration in Plotinus: 'Thus it is by transcending the world that Plotinus's divine principles are a source of perfection in the world, so the two birds, precisely by departing from the world, become its *angeloi*; the lovers, by living towards the fulfillment of their love in death, provide a "patterne of love" for the world they leave behind.' (p. 219).
The Platonists of the Renaissance could be similarly drawn on. Pico commenting on Benivieni wrote: '[Men] Their onely means of release from this bondage is the amatory life; which by sensible beauties, exciting in the soul a remembrance of the intellectual, raiseth her from this terrene life to the eternal; by the flame of love refined into an Angel.' (*A Platonick*

Discourse upon Love, tr. Thomas Stanley, ed. E. G. Gardner, Boston, 1914, p. 17—I. xii).

Pico refers to Plato in the *Timaeus* where it is said that God 'Soweth and scattereth Souls, some in the Moon, others in other Planets and Stars, the Instruments of Time.' (p. 74—III. vii).

Ficino expatiates upon how love and the beautiful transform the soul, and in observing how it is proper to speak of God as fire—since fire purges—and the soul, loved by God, becomes diaphanous, and separated from the body it takes on a divine light—'amor uerò deificat'. (*In Platonem*, *Argumentum in Sextam Epistolam*; Opera [1576], II, 1533–4).

Much in the poem does indeed suggest that Truth, Beautie, Constancie, and Love are eternal entities, not only the exemplars but the informing principles of the Phoenix and Turtle, and that these two, when passed from the earth, act in just this way for those who remain. It is accordingly reasonable to refer the sense of this line to the other meanings that in treating of the nature of the spiritual world would harmonize with this interpretation. But precise explication of the terms is elusive. If, for example, one should attempt to argue that the 'starres' signify the stellar deities of Plato, or the star-gods of the Stoics, that very preciseness would introduce an alien element into what we can be fairly confident of in the poem. If the word 'Co-supremes' should be taken to be a reference to the relation of the members of the Trinity, that would introduce an outrageous meaning as long as it seems that the two birds stand for humans. Nor, I think, could one properly appeal to Plotinus': 'to be a god is to be integral with the Supreme' (VI. 9. 8). And similarly, 'starres' and 'Co-supremes' do not seem to be quite congruent with exemplars, or Ideas.

There is a certain way in which meanings may be given these terms that would cohere with what is scholastic in the poem as well as with what is Platonic and, more particularly, with what is Platonic in Saint Thomas and the pseudo-Dionysius. And since their reasoning does seem to be useful in interpreting other meanings in the poem it may not be wholly impertinent to refer to them on this matter.

The fundamental conception is expressed by the pseudo-Dionysius: 'But hereafter, when we are incorruptible and immortal, and attain the blessed lot of being like unto Christ, then (as the Scripture saith), we shall be forever with the Lord, fulfilled with His visible Theophany in holy contemplations, the which shall shine about us with radiant beams of glory (even as once of old it shone around the Disciples at the Divine Transfiguration); and so shall we, with our mind made passionless and spiritual, participate in a spiritual illumination from Him, and in an union transcending our mental faculties, and there, amidst the blinding blissful impulsions of His dazzling rays, we shall, in a diviner manner than at present, be like unto the heavenly Intelligences. For, as the infallible

Scripture saith, we shall be equal to the angels and shall be the Sons of God, being Sons of the Resurrection.' (*On The Divine Names*, tr. Rolf, I. 4 (p. 58)—592C).

Being equal to the angels—*issaggeloi*—'celestial essences'—these souls have for their 'mission' 'the transmitting of the illumination and the spiritual perfection they have themselves received from God'. (*Celestial Hierarchies*, 261 c).

The highest of the celestial orders are the seraphim—'the burning ones'—and to these—'supremis angelis' (*S.S.* q.180. a.5 ob.1)—the revelation from God is immediate. It is these who through their influence effect the purification of others: 'For just as God purifies all essences in that degree in which he is the very cause of purification, they do this in making His providence available to those who make themselves accessible to it.' (*Celestial Hierarchies*, 308A). 'Worthy in the highest degree of entering into communion with God and in cooperation the seraphim imitate as far as they are able to the beauty of the powers and works of God.' (212 B-C).

As a final comment, I myself find little of use in noticing Shakespeare's other uses of the word *supreme*, but, for reasons I do not understand, the Schmidt *Lexikon* defines Shakespeare's meaning as 'the life of purity'.

[30] *In Librum Beati Dionysii De Divinis Nominibus Expositio*, ed. Ceslai Pera, Turin, 1950, p. 148 (C. IV. 1. xi [450]).

In this commentary Saint Thomas stresses the divine initiative, what does not permit lovers simply to love themselves, that takes them outside themselves in ecstasy—they are the lovers of that of which they are loved. This is *amativus motus*. (p. 147-449). And by how much the more perfect the love, the more perfect the union that proceeds from it.

This *circulatio* is stressed by Proclus. (*The Elements of Theology*, ed. E. R. Dodds, Oxford, 1933, pp. 35-37). The idea is as important to Boethius as to the pseudo-Dionysius, and in Dante we see it developed at the very center of the story of Beatrice and God's working through her. (J. A. Mazzeo, 'Plato's Eros and Dante's Amore', *Traditio*, XII [1956], 327-31).

'Love . . . is spiritual union. The soul loves itself and other things, and increasingly as "goodness" appears to it, in or outside itself, in the ways and degrees suggested. But, in the last analysis, what is goodness but fulness of being? And what, concretely, is this but God, who spans infinity in one act? [*Convivio* 4.9.3] So we return to our definition of love as spiritual union of soul and thing, soul and self, soul and soul; which, taken up into the absolute, is the pre-containing unity of the divine mind. Hence God *is* love. Hence the deepest orientation of the created spirit is to no abstract *summum bonum*, but to the primary love itself. When all is said, what the soul finally loves is love; or rather, a Lover; no passive object, but an active ardour that runs to meet us:

> Quello infinito e ineffabil bene
> che la su è, così corre ad amore
> com' a lucido corpo raggio vene. (*Purg.* XV, 67–69).'

(Kenelm Foster, 'The Mind in Love: Dante's Philosophy', *Aquinas Society of London Papers*, No. 25 [1956], 19–20).

[31] The conception is as important to Plato as to Plotinus. In Christian thought it is defined by Saint Augustine, *De Trinitate*, 6,7. Saint Thomas said, 'God is altogether simple'. (*S.T.* I. q.3. a.7).

Ficino says, 'God is not only the most simple, He is simplicity itself.' (*In Dionysium Areopagitam de Divinis nominibus*, in *Opera* [1576], II, 1025).

[32] It may be useful to mention here a single aspect of the scholastic doctrine of immortality:

'. . . when the human body ceases to be actuated by its soul it disintegrates and man himself likewise ceases to be. But the act of being does not enter the composition of the essence of the soul as if its function were to make it to be a soul; its effect is not to make it to be a soul, it is to cause the essence of the soul to be a being.'

(Étienne Gilson, *Elements of Christian Philosophy*, New York, 1959, p. 212).

[33] See above, p. 48.

[34] 'An Anatomy of "The Phoenix and the Turtle",' *Shakespeare Survey*, 15 (1962), 104, 107.

[35] (From the Introduction to *Plotinus, The Enneads*, tr. Stephen MacKenna 2nd ed. rev. B. S. Page, London, 1956, pp. xlix-li).

[36] *Des Fureurs Héroïques*, ed. P.-H. Michel, Paris, 1954 (*Prima Parte, Dialogo* I), p. 141.

[37] *Prima Parte, Dialogo* III, pp. 191, 189.

[38] *A Platonick Discourse upon Love*, tr. Thomas Stanley, ed, E. G. Gardner, Boston, 1914, p. 44.

[39] Donald Guss, 'Donne's Petrarchism', *Journal of English and Germanic Philology*, LXIV (1965), 27.

[40] Jean Trouillard, *La Purification Plotinienne*, Paris, 1955, p. 101.

The Spirit of the Occasion

A Midsummer Night's Dream is like the loveliest of songs, ordered, whole, clear and radiant.[1] It is as rich in meaning, and understanding how much it is all of a piece we see in it the witness of a superlative art, an art as like nature's as we hear spoken of in a later play in praise of one of the most admired of heroines—

> When you dance, I wish you
> A wave of the sea, that you might ever do
> Nothing but that, move still, still so,
> And own no other function.
> (*The Winter's Tale*, IV. iv. 140–3)

Often it is the mere naming of things that gives us the idea of perfection—the woosel-cock with orange-tawny bill, the finch, the sparrow, and the lark—but often, too, it is the world as those in the play see it, as they recognize in the beauty of nature the beauty of their own natures, most especially in what allies them to other creatures in the ways of desire and fruition. The first words make the moon into someone knowing well enough the feelings of the lovers she is shining on:

> O, methinks, how slow
> This old moon wanes! She lingers my desires,
> Like to a stepdame or a dowager,
> Long withering out a young man's revenue.

Hippolyta speaks even more feelingly of the world and of time as sentient beings like her lover and herself, participants in their dreams:

85

> Four days will quickly steep themselves in night,
> Four nights will quickly dream away the time;
> And then the moon, like to a silver bow
> New-bent in heaven, shall behold the night
> Of our solemnities.

But it is not only a certain sympathy the world is imagined to show for the loves of humans that keeps before us the idea of the correspondences of order and beauty everywhere and that accounts for the fluency of the work. The drama proceeds, of course, through a variety of actions, there are hindrances and stumbling-blocks to the purest ambitions, yet in the disjunctions of the plot and the fallings-out of lovers, in the very disorders, we sense the same charming power overlooking matters as in the wooings. The words that describe wretchedness make even that wonderful—

> No night is now with hymn or carol blest ...
> The seasons alter. Hoary-headed frosts
> Fall in the fresh lap of the crimson rose. ...
> (II. i. 102, 107–8)

The world has lost its ancient innocence, the time is no longer holy, yet the poetry holds the white frosts and the red roses in such honor we know that all is far from ruined, and we see that mortals, too, whatever their disruptions, still deserve love and wonder.

The indication that so much is taking place by moonlight accounts for much. The moon enhances all it shines on and its loveliness almost redeems strife. It makes that which is beautiful in itself into something exquisite. It changes reflections on water into the image of a goddess—

> when Phoebe doth behold
> Her silver visage in the watery glass.
> (I. i. 209–10)

When the moon scatters dew we see it as liquid pearl.(211) The beauty is as winning as the humor in the picture concluding

86

Bottom's play, 'Moonshine and Lion are left to bury the dead.'
(V. i. 334)

The entire work is rich with images that transform the world
we ordinarily see. Often this happens through the attribution of
perfection:

> Things base and vile, holding no quantity,
> Love can transpose to form and dignity. (I. i. 232–3)

Sometimes a word or thought will re-create the beauty moonlight
confers upon the familiar. Love and the moon are always
discovering the precious, and in the dark, it seems, sight and love
become one—

> It is not night when I do see your face. (II. i. 221)

And thus, all the while the play proceeds so fancifully, it
reminds us of experiences we have known in life, it keeps us in
touch with what we know we are right to cherish even in preserv-
ing such detachment as the fantastic world of the play insists
upon. But the richest effect and the one leading to the most
rewarding delight is achieved rather more indirectly. As we meet
with one change after another—fear as well as love confusing and
misleading now this one, now that; magic forcing inexplicable
exchanges; light itself transforming tragedy—the moon peering
through a chink in a wall—it is as if we were seeing in change the
face of life itself, and life as beauty.

From the beginning, in the language and in the action of the
play, everything points to change—the changes love effects, the
alterations of magic, the moon's mutations. Ointments and
enchantments are but bringing about more extravagant metamorphoses than love and moonlight would if left to themselves—

> Be it ounce or cat or bear,
> Pard, or boar with bristled hair,
> In thy eye that shall appear
> When thou wak'st, it is thy dear.
>
> (II. ii. 30–3)

In the distant past it was the Duke and the Amazon, now it is the lovers and artisans and even the fairies who find themselves receiving forms they do not recognize as their own, love and hate and magic playing with them as winds with leaves. Often it must have seemed that whirl was king, that there was nothing but misrule and anarchy. There was in fact the awful suggestion that the very seasons may have fallen out of order, yet, as the language continues to remind us with its beauty, the wonder is no more dimmed for the tempest-tossed than for us. Indeed, least of all for us in the audience, for whom it is never possible to think that love and magic and elvish spirits are only making mischief.

To begin with, our sympathies are with almost everyone. Then, the first words of the Duke had won us over, however fleetingly, to the thought that time and nature and the moon were in league with the lovers. When we add to this the charm of the heroines, the gallantry of the men, the virtues of the artisans, the awesomeness of the fairies—so delicate we can hardly believe they would be the cause of lasting woe—we are as certain as we wish to be of a happy outcome. But there are other grounds as well to warrant our expectations, these in the nature of the changes.

The movements from loving to misery, from self-containment to intoxication, the violence in the language of an offended girl, the lavishness of the adulations of a fairy queen, all this has not only the energy but the beauty of Spenser's Mutabilitie, 'That could the greatest wrath soone turne to grace.' The persons in the play are in constant motion, flight and pursuit set the tempo from the beginning to all but the end:

> He goes before me, and still dares me on:
> When I come where he calls, then he is gone.
> The villain is much lighter-heeled than I.
> I followed fast, but faster he did fly,
> That fallen am I in dark uneven way,
> And here will rest me. (III. ii. 413–18)

Lysander now falls asleep, and the next instant Demetrius is there to fall asleep beside him, then Helena, too, then Hermia, and when they awaken Puck's charms have changed things once again. In what in production asks for lyrical, choreographic movements, the transformations in their beauty as in their nature are as alive with humor as with the *slancio* of love.

The very air, we are told, is as crowded with life—

> night's swift dragons cut the clouds full fast,
> And yonder shines Aurora's harbinger;
> At whose approach ghosts, wand'ring here and there,
> Troop home to churchyards: damnèd spirits all,
> That in crossways and floods have burial,
> Already to their wormy beds are gone.
>
> (III. ii. 379–84)

All the concurrences are strangely ordered—Venus fortunately absent at a certain time, ghosts at rest when other business can go forward, the magic ointment applied to the wrong lover although ultimately to the right end, Titania's waking to look upon and love the perfect foil. The suddenness with which so much takes place, the rousings and subsidings in all their variety, are as wonderful as the changes themselves, and indeed it is the ease and swiftness of the transformations that signify most plainly the role in life of love and imagination and thought. Puck said he could girdle the globe in forty minutes, love changes as swiftly for Demetrius, a mere phrase extends the vistas of thought into the unending. Faced with what is evidently an inexhaustible disposition to change, we are dissuaded from supposing there is ever to be rest, least of all for the discouraged. And yet in these continuing metamorphoses and alterations there is apparent an undeniable direction. Life like thought continues to discover new forms; nothing disintegrates. The confusion that leads to despair ends in hope, the distorted becomes fit. All goes to show that the power in change in the world of this play at least, and in this way of looking at the most wretched entanglements of humans, is the power to confer grace. This is why, I think, at the end when there are promises of resolution and serenity, when it is said that underlying all is an admirable constancy, we can believe it, having seen in change so much of the disposition to perfection.

Theseus was to speak of love and poetry as equal in their force to frenzy. The happenings in the lives not only of those in the mechanicals' play bear him out—almost every person appears to exist to be impetuous, and events themselves come about as suddenly and as it were incoherently. If from time to time we believe the humans are quite out of control we may even think some blind force is driving them. We may even think of fate— certainly the sense of powerlessness that overcomes the bemused lovers suggests that. But then, as hope to satisfy the heart's desire is reborn again and again, this other thought reasserts itself, so that when finally Hippolyta expresses so magically what all along we had been depending on, we find ourselves sharing her confidence—

> the story of the night told over,
> And all their minds transfigured so together,
> More witnesseth than fancy's images,
> And grows to something of great constancy.
>
> (V. i. 23–6)

The imagery transfixes similarly the changes of nature. The light and shading are so distinct we seem ourselves to have been brought into a Botticelli spring so to speak, into just such a flowered world. The quickness of the winds of March is the very spirit of the scene, enthralling us for itself even as we see the persons we have come to care about brought to a wretched state. The words touch us so intimately, indeed, that we are induced to accept this fairy world as our own, and as we become aware of this we conclude this is no mere charming, we have been persuaded, rather, that this is indeed the world we know. What we are seeing as we sometimes fail to is that the same transmuting power that is at work in the loves of those in the play and in the honoring of speech is at work in the world itself. What we see as motion and as change is that fanciful story accounting for the streaks in a flower—

> a little western flower,
> Before milk-white, now purple with love's wound,
>   (II. i. 166–7)

we see as well in 'the fierce vexation of a dream' (IV. i. 72), and in the progress of thought:

> The wildest hath not such a heart as you.
> Run when you will. The story shall be changed:
> Apollo flies, and Daphne holds the chase;
> The dove pursues the griffin; the mild hind
> Makes speed to catch the tiger—bootless speed,
> When cowardice pursues, and valor flies.
>   (II. i. 229–34)

We see beauty even in the transfer of loves—

> Fare thee well, nymph. Ere he do leave this grove,
> Thou shalt fly him, and he shall seek thy love.
>   (II. i. 245–6)

What we are recognizing as motion and change in this world that has come into our possession is that same movement towards perfection we know in the world away from Athens, gracing the waves of the sea. It is the grace inherent in love and in the formings of the mind, discovering perfection now in Helena, now in Hermia, even in the thought of the world's decay. It is the power that lends even despair a grace to redeem it.

> Tell true, even for my sake!
> Durst thou have looked upon him being awake?
> And hast thou killed him sleeping? O brave touch!
> Could not a worm, an adder, do so much?
> An adder did it; for with doubler tongue
> Than thine, thou serpent, never adder stung.
>   (III. ii. 68–73)

To those lost and confused in the woods chance and misfortune are as arbitrary as the collocations in dreams and in the fancy, but nothing is formless—Bottom's most unmanageable thoughts discover the most felicitous of words.

The powers working in every aspect of change show that there is but one manner through which things come into being and pass away. There are the same processes in nature as in dreams. Knowing enough to marvel we discover the fitness in all change, discovering something like reason guiding each movement, determining form and grace—as in the joining of an ass's head to a man's body, and this particular man's; turning reflections on the water into the face of a goddess; exulting with Puck—

> Sometime a horse I'll be, sometime a hound,
> A hog, a headless bear, sometime a fire.
> (III. i. 97–8)

Wilson Knight observed that the images and distortions that are so repelling in *Macbeth*—spotted snakes with double tongue, beetles black and worms and snails—have become lovely in this play.[2] In the tragedy ugliness is the essence the imagination discovers in its own corruption. In *A Midsummer Night's Dream* deformity has become a game for the imagination not in corrupting but in honoring love and thereby discovering good. Airy nothings take on the forms of nature, nature accepts the forms imagination gives it as belonging to it, everything turns happily into something else with the joy of life itself in reaching perfection. The compositions of fear dissolve in the fancy that created them to become wonders, the dream fades, truth lightens. In his confusion Bottom can allow himself to think that 'reason and love keep little company together nowadays' (III. i. 129–30); others will say that reason, though confounded, saw division grow together.

A Midsummer Night's Dream commences in announcing the ceremony that is to unite Theseus with an Amazon he has defeated in battle. A play is to be part of the festivities but first we shall be seeing one in which they themselves are involved. The nature of Theseus' conquest of Hippolyta is Shakespeare's addition to the ancient story, as if to tell us that the changes in the affections of the lovers in the play are no more violently ruinous than that of these two who have come into so rich a happiness.

In speaking of the few days remaining until the wedding Theseus and Hippolyta are enjoying the assurance that belongs to those who believe the world itself must be favoring the harmony that is now theirs:

> Now, fair Hippolyta, our nuptial hour
> Draws on apace. Four happy days bring in
> Another moon. . . .

Hippolyta concludes the implicit promise—

> And then the moon, like to a silver bow
> New-bent in heaven, shall behold the night
> Of our solemnities.

All hazards having run their course, they are saying, they may confidently await the future, and they allow themselves to think of time and nature and the goddess of mutability herself as in league with them. So Theseus, in what is for him only partly a fanciful thought, complains—

> how slow
> This old moon wanes! She lingers my desires,
> Like to a stepdame or a dowager,
> Long withering out a young man's revenue.

Hippolyta makes it all seem a single life the two of them share with time and the moon—

> Four days will quickly steep themselves in night;
> Four nights will quickly dream away the time.

It is not, I think, simply time and the moon's magic they are praising, even though they count on them to effect their fulfilment. They are attending solemnities, and they are honoring the power that enables oaths to outlast dreams.

A tangled history and a fierce courtship lay behind the rich assurance and the miraculous words on constancy Hippolyta was to utter as the play draws to its end. But before we are to hear the blessing implicit in 'the story of the night told over' (V. i. 23), the play we are to see presents us with a succession of infidelities and

93

rages like those Theseus and Hippolyta had known. Before
Theseus had brought Hippolyta home as his captive he had loved
and broken off with Perigenia, Aegles, Ariadne, and another
Amazon, Antiopa. There may even have been an affair with
Titania. As for Hippolyta, Oberon said she had been the mistress
of Theseus. Helena and Hermia were to experience no greater
reversals. There was also the turbulence in the love of the king
and queen of the fairies. And so when we are so taken with the
lovely assurance in those first words, and the firm assertion at
the end—

> all their minds transfigured so together—
>
> (V. i. 24)

we know that all this—the passing of the time for the Duke and
Hippolyta as well as the troubles of the others—is the snatching of
hope and faith out of 'the jaws of darkness' (I. i. 148). I think this
is how we are to regard the play before us, the representation of a
marvellous rescue, and the richness of the pleasure—'dreaming
away the time'—is the means humans have of overcoming terror
at the thought of the loss of love.

'The story of the night' includes the loves of Theseus and
Hippolyta, their troubles are being repeated, and in that repeating
of the confusions inherent in the attachments of love all proceeds
as in the implacable sense of dreams. The conclusion here will
follow as it does for one in a later play:

> Full many a lady
> I have eyed with best regard, and many a time
> Th' harmony of their tongues hath into bondage
> Brought my too diligent ear; for several virtues
> Have I liked several women; never any
> With so full soul but some defect in her
> Did quarrel with the noblest grace she owed,
> And put it to the foil; but you, O you,
> So perfect and so peerless, are created
> Of every creature's best. (*The Tempest*, III. i. 39–48)

The past was prologue, the dreams in the troubled sleep rehearsals, out of which takes form the knowledge of a splendor that will repel the dark.

It is the sense that mortals are powerless before what has been strangely determined that the main action extends our idea of harmony, even perhaps a union, between the power at work in the love Theseus and Hippolyta are celebrating and the forces working in nature that the cycle of the moon and the processes of fruition everywhere make manifest and that the powers troubling dreams also attest to. In this sense of a two-fold agency the action of the drama is proceeding as sequences do in dreams, so much that is impossibly strange somehow accommodated to a single process. The surprises the lovers face, the unimaginable refusals and betrayals, the birth of new passions, follow in such illogic as we are fascinated by in dreams where our sense of the ineluctable goes hand in hand with the fear of what ought never to happen but does, the inconceivable part of the course of things. And the audience, seeing the misfortunes and the final compositions of the loves, knows it is observing in the misadventures of these others just such matters as have troubled Theseus and Hippolyta, that they are in fact just such troubles as haunt all dreaming and all love, and so there is, we understand, the character of the accommodation between the fears and charms of dreams with the promise humans keep making themselves and that nature keeps making for us.

I think what is chiefly harmonizing the various actions is not a system of contrasts in arranging a thematic development, but a conception referring the contentment love promises to the excitement we feel at the coming of the spring winds. The contentment is in accord with nature, and nature has its own contentment, ordered by still other lovely powers. As the play has it, the moon graces even in its obscuring, and each change—in how things seem and in how they are—and each passage of love and fortune, even each destined event, points to an abiding benevolence such as we learn of in these brief glimpses of Venus and Diana, but most of all in Bottom's remembrance of his dream, a world beyond change.

In such a conception of the play, the beginning and ending

95

scenes would be not so much a frame for the main adventures as a key to how we are to regard them, and indeed what we are to make of the title, the play being called a 'Dream'. Coleridge may have meant just this when he remarked, 'I am convinced that Shakespeare availed himself of the title of this play in his own mind, and worked upon it as a dream throughout, but especially, and, perhaps, unpleasingly, in this broad determination of ingrateful treachery in Helena, so undisguisedly avowed to herself, and this, too, after the witty, cool philosophizing that precedes.'[3]

I am unable to decipher all Coleridge may have meant in the second part of his sentence, but I think the meaning of the first part, extended, would support the conclusions I am drawing. The grounds of fear in love are as real, as transient, and as insubstantial as those in dreams, and accordingly in setting our hearts on others we are driven to the usual confounding, not knowing which is which, dream or reality, the glorious one herself or our love for her, not knowing well enough to distinguish truth from lies. And so the souls are buffeted, now here, now there, and they love and learn that their most certain hopes are one with the passing of time and the changes of the moon and coming into being and passing away, and that something always abides.

So it is that all that happens is presented to us as at once capricious and fated, the fated shown as the caprice of wanton elves, the capricious as the ineluctable tyranny of nature and of drugs working upon nature. It is not so much that all is other than it seems as that what is happening we know on the instant to be both inevitable and not to be accounted for. We milk meanings from the paradoxes, of course, but our pleasure is in the strangeness and the implications of the changes. It is this contradictoriness in treating with the impossible that Shakespeare exploits in continually referring us to dreams and moonlight and what we think of them, showing how even in what we recognize as false, even in the incoherent, the radiance of beauty all the while reveals the constant guidance of the powers at work in all these changes.

Much of our interest and pleasure arises in noticing the slightness of the disjunctions, the minuteness of the omissions that distinguish the false from the true, the real from the apparent, as it also is in dreams. Such focus and brilliance shine upon what is brought before us, the images are so distinct and bright that they possess the vividness of the authentic, their falsity revealed, when it is, only by an incoherence in the consequence, or a feature missing from its habitual ambience. There belongs a special beauty, it appears, to the barely demonstrably false—which is to say, to that feature not only of any dream but of any metaphor which reminds us of the differences it negates—

> The ox hath therefore stretched his yoke in vain,
> The ploughman lost his sweat, and the green corn
> Hath rotted ere his youth attained a beard. (II. i. 93–5)

When those differences reside primarily in the attachment of human qualities, some suggestion of a person in the non-human, there comes before us always the sense of the valuing of life, the wonder and excellence in our own lives we are so glad to recognize in others and elsewhere. Or there appears on the contrary the very opposite, the fear of an invincible power thwarting the natural course of things, thwarting the meaningful and benevolent everywhere—

> my love to Hermia,
> Melted as the snow, seems to me now
> As the remembrance of an idle gaud,
> Which in my childhood I did dote upon. (IV. i. 164–7)

There comes to mind now an idea of the loveliness of youth and of the melting snow, and there is as much to wonder at in the feared as in the loved, as much to wonder at in the unliving snow as in the passing of life.

In the dark all is obscured, Puck mistakes his prey, lovers mistake each other. The dark would make everything inexplicable yet we are persuaded all has happened as it had to. The ointment was misapplied but its effects were as intended. A charm makes a fairy queen love blindly. A mischievous spirit changes a man naturally given to the truest prose into a creature of the silliest fantasy. So whether magic functions perfectly or character changes preposterously, all happens as it seems it must, and it is in this that the strangeness lies. In this remarkable conception the natural and the preposterous are alike authentic. Since we never mistake which is which, we are never tempted to reduce all this to fate, to some certifiable demonstration that all follows from determined causes in predictable sequence. And yet, just as in dreams, all is heavy with the sense that this is as it had to be.

There is the same deceptiveness in dreams where also we are moved by the sense of fatality, where the sense of the inescapable is the very means of our mesmerizing. Only in dreams, where there is no pretense that the causes are understood, the idea of the inescapable obviously goes beyond whatever suggestions of a cause there are. But in the resemblance to suggestions of fatality in dreams with the way things are presented in *A Midsummer Night's Dream*—on the one hand, in the assurance that there are specific causes for the strange happenings; on the other, that the results are out of all proportion to the causes—we are discovering the central paradox of the play's ordering and poise. We have been induced to regard facts as if they were dreams and dreams as if they were facts, to believe that there are no mysteries to the ways things happen and that the strangest events are perfectly explicable. In leading us to play this way with truth Shakespeare entertains us by showing how closely dreams skirt the truth, how great is the attraction of the false, and in this complicated confounding of illusion and assurance, every time, like Helena or Hermia or any of them, we find ourselves clinging to truth and committing ourselves to it, we learn that it is truth that is eluding us. It is not only our senses that are misleading, or the imagination conjuring up goddesses or bears. When we have learned that the dream is bottomless, we have learned that reality is.

Theseus and Hippolyta are but stewards in a world ruled over by Oberon and Titania and their henchmen. They have worked out their own fortunes independently of magic, and although in the distant past it has been said that they two had dealings with these capricious powers, they now function freely, and offer themselves up freely, and as freely go to their rest. How much, in their helpless state, they will need the ministerings of the immortals—or, for that matter, of Puck sweeping out the corners—we are left to guess for ourselves. They, at least, are composed. They are counting on an assurance, a matter of great constancy, that neither fancy nor reason has knowledge of, before which fate itself will be powerless. The passage to that fulfilment has been a long one.

The first words of Theseus and Hippolyta had told of a few days yet to come in the rich and decorous anticipation of their marriage, celebrating the time the moon's course was measuring. Then, all but lost in their contentment, they were interrupted by a father's suit, appealing to the Duke to enforce his right to choose a husband for his daughter. The image of the peaceful flow of time had broken and the audience now finds itself attending to a series of troublesome matters. There are changes of scene, from the court to the country, engagements are broken off, new attachments confuse matters further, there are flights and pursuits and the play of tempestuous feelings. The initial calm is replaced by turmoil although the show of distress does not press upon us as heavily as it might for all takes place in settings of stunning beauty and the speakers are as conscious of the exquisiteness of flowers and woods and streams and of the moon's light as they are of their distress.

Then, after the first interruption and the flights of the lovers to the wood near Athens, there is the introduction of persons of a very different kind. A party of workmen has been engaged to help in the festivities for the Duke's marriage, and in passing through the wood they have encountered some supernatural creatures who are intervening in the affairs of the lovers. The plainness and insensitivity of Bottom and his friends mock the ecstasies of the lovers as much as in their simple seriousness they mock their desperation. They mock the high-flown thoughts and gorgeous imaginings as well, and love and poetry, too, even though in their own way they pay honor to these:

> The raging rocks
> And shivering shocks
> Shall break the locks
>   Of prison gates;
> And Phibbus' car
> Shall shine from far,
> And make and mar
>   The foolish Fates.
>   (I. ii. 24–31)

Bottom and his companions will return several times as the preparations for the marriage progress, and the comment their plainness will always make upon the romancing and philosophizing and poetry of the others weaves a certain pattern of meaning while still other ideas are coming forward with the intrusion of supernatural beings. But nothing carries such a sting as that most guileless of epithets, the 'foolish' Fates—the powers that are so all-conquering, so heedless, and in the end so ineffectual. The young lovers we first met have no sooner eloped than they become separated, two other young lovers have added their complicating interests, happy arrangements are upset, lovers are abandoned, loves are misdirected. Yet when the confusion and distress have gone about as far as they can, it will be these same mistakings, worked on by the supernatural beings that will straighten out the troubles, and we shall be returned to many of the imaginings with which the play began, about the benevolence of time and the happy conspirings of the moon with the desires of lovers. The conclusion ends in richness greater than before, for there is harmony now not only between the pairs of young people but the king and queen of the fairies have reconciled their differences, and neither reason nor dreaming will measure their contentment.

The play ends with Puck sweeping the stage. The fanciful and elaborate goings-on are over with, dancing and music have wound up the festivities, the wedding parties are off to bed and the audience too is being sent home. We are being given once more that conventional and charming send-off where the persons in the play, the actors, and all the others in the theater are being addressed at the same time. But just before the last words—

good-night unto you all—

there is a reminder of what is immediately ahead for everyone, now that it is all over, the palace dark, the theater dark, the players departed. The empty world is being left to the powers of mischief, and out of the darkness, out of the graves and tombs, evil spirits will be rising, they will be taking over, and this is why Oberon and Titania, and Puck sweeping out every corner, aim to keep mischief away from the lovers who have just found their happy conclusions. Charms are uttered to protect those who are asleep, and even those who are being conceived are to be protected from the curses of moles and harelips. Were it not for these good spirits—Puck is saying—

following darkness like a dream—

there is no telling what might happen there is so much still to fear.

At first thought this might seem a strange reminder following the marriage entertainment that has just concluded the play although it fits well enough with much that has troubled the minds of the young persons caught up in adventure in a wood near Athens. Much has taken place by moonlight, and there has been such loveliness in the scene and in the poetry, there is such happiness in prospect for the lovers, and there has been as well such richness in the thought, we might have expected more like a blessing on being dismissed from the theater. The happiness we have just been witnessing and sharing is such we can hardly take seriously the intrusion of evil or mischief at this point, but we are respectful enough of old wives' wisdom not to object. Nevertheless, the pairings we have been attending to are so full of happy promise that the suggestions of fear and trouble arouse little concern in us, and, besides, Puck's earnestness in sweeping out the corners comically relieves us of any great burden. We enjoy watching him much as we enjoy a child's seriousness in coping with something fearful he has dreamed up. We have arrived safely in harbor.

Yet when we think of it, much that has happened in the play has taken place quite as portentously as the ills the good fairy seem to fear, and certainly to Hermia and Helena and Demetrius and Lysander life once had certainly been nightmarish. But more than that, so much of what happened had been the work of creatures if not as constantly mischievous as those Puck is speaking of, yet they made trouble those other mischievous spirits would have been delighted to cause. We have been more than a little prepared to think that what has been offered to our view as a representation of something like the troubles of lovers in life is not very much different from the strange life that takes over when the world's asleep and mischief is free to do its work, free, to trouble dreams—

> Whilst the heavy ploughman snores,
> All with weary task fordone;
>   (V. i. 356–7)

like the flies Mercutio speaks of walking across the noses of sleeping men, free to start some at once vast although for all that sometimes inconsequential cataclysms. Like the creatures the old wives believe in.

Bottom thought he had been dreaming, and in speaking of his enchantment so but in words that make us think he is not far from an intuition of the foundation of all being, he collects for us the thoughts the play has stirred in us about the ways in which men and women are made fools of, and so suggestively that his words become what we ourselves are often willing to use in speaking of our own existence. And so from many sides, from the events, from Bottom's words, from what Theseus says about fancy and lunacy and love and poetry, the play has been entertaining us with innumerable ways of looking at life as if it were a dream, making us wonder if reality and dream are not forever masking as the other. We are so charmed with the ingeniousness of the devices and the beauty and wisdom of the poetry and the splendor of the spectacle that we are easily persuaded it would be a wise man who could be sure in such a world what was the true state of things and what the false, and what the causes of evil are, spirits or ourselves. There is more to it, of course, than the charm of the fanciful, and even than the amusement we take in the confusion, for there is sharp pain, and while the note does not sound often enough to bring us up short, yet in Hermia's—

> Am I not Hermia? Are not you Lysander?
> I am as fair now as I was erewhile.
> Since night you loved me; yet since night you left me.
> When, then, you left me. (O, the gods forbid!)
> In earnest, shall I say?— (III. ii. 273-7)

there is the seed of such grief as Lear knows—

> Look with thine ears: see how yond justice rails
> upon yond simple thief. Hark, in thine ear.
> Change places, and, handy-dandy, which is the
> justice, which is the thief? (IV. vi. 150-4)

The note in the last speeches and the charms of Oberon and Titania and Puck are indeed something more than comments on a play and a dream coming to an end, they tell, however lightly, of fears and the grounds of all fear, the true grounds. They speak of so much that sense thinks unaccountable that we see clearly now that what was weaving in and out of all those misprisions and misunderstandings that led to quarrels and betrayals, was the fear it is the nature of what is unaccountable to engender. It is this that dreams and actuality have in common, the very occasions of love and hate in life as in dreams arising from causes we shall never be able to search out, neither to exorcise once and for all, nor to respect enough. We do know that fears are often the parents of dreams, and in this play we are further told that there is indeed danger in the confusion that has come upon all things in the dark backward and abysm of time—

> Therefore the winds, piping to us in vain,
> As in revenge, have sucked up from the sea
> Contagious fogs: which falling in the land
> Hath every pelting river made so proud
> That they have overborne their continents. . . .

> The spring, the summer,
> The childing autumn, angry winter, change
> Their wonted liveries; and the mazèd world,
> By their increase, now knows not which is which.
>
> (II. i. 88–92, 111–14)

The quarrel between Oberon and Titania has been the cause of this—'We are their parents and original' (117). The quarrel was rooted in old jealousies, the very lovers for whom the play of Pyramus is to be presented, Theseus and Hippolyta, having been once their favorites, and in accusing each other of wanton crimes in once leading Theseus to break faith, and Hippolyta to have been the love of Oberon, they say that to these fallings-off are to be traced the inroads of chaos into the very order of nature. In their words we see some signs that they wish to re-establish their first harmoniousness, there is the accusation that their present enmities are 'the forgeries of jealousy' (81) which is to say, unfounded—but there is also a real cause of dissension, over the possession of a changeling boy, a mortal, whom Oberon would take from Titania to be his. Thus we perceive that what is at the root of the fears of the mortal lovers in the play is what is at the root of the trouble of the fairies and is the original cause of the present state of the world, fear of the loss of the beloved, lost in fact from causes that were forged. It is the betrayal of love that has brought about these dreams, these forgeries, and it is once more the fear of the loss of love, this time of the changeling, that maintains the fairies in their madness. And the changes, the thrashings about, the troublings in sleep, as poetry and love, are the activities of the power that would reverse betrayal.

The reason we accept the warnings at the end as happily as we do, why the talk about the scattering of evil spirits is so happy a send-off, is that we are persuaded that the causes of falling-out are illusions. We have agreed to share the playfulness of the idea that our own fears can be exorcised, and what we know is that the world began a long time ago, and that when one story ends, another begins. But we are also told to wait, to anticipate something transcending the unstable world of forgery and betrayal, to count on 'something of great constancy'. We are glad to comply.

I do not believe we are to take Coleridge's remark that Shakespeare worked on this play as a dream 'throughout' to mean that the play is just such a representation that Christopher Sly dreamed up, or that we are to take it all as passing before us like Bottom's dreaming. The initial circumstances are presented to us quite patently as taking place at an ascertainable court, and there is never an indication that we are to take what follows as other than a sequence of happenings in a world we recognize as like ours. There are romantic and preposterous matters aplenty, but the effort is to present the impossible as all-too possible, and while we may not accept the fairies, the ointments, the transformation of Bottom as actualities of the kind we credit when we see parents setting down cruel conditions for lovers and lovers changing affections overnight, the unreal is offered to us with the circumstantiality, not of dreams where the air of mysteriousness overlays the particulars, but with the matter-of-factness we expect of a world in which, when we have need of a pharmacist, we receive the most precise directions:

> crush this herb into Lysander's eye,
> Whose liquor hath this virtuous property,
> To take from thence all error with his might,
> And make his eyeballs roll with wonted sight.
>
> (III. ii. 366–9)

This same particularity gives the stamp of dreadful authenticity to the account of the original falling-out of Oberon and Titania, the preposterous cause of the impossible as well as of the probable happenings in a world like ours in some of its mishapings:

> The ox hath therefore stretched his yoke in vain,
> The ploughman lost his sweat, and the green corn
> Hath rotted ere his youth attained a beard;
> The fold stands empty in the drowned field,
> And crows are fatted with the murrion flock.
>
> (II. i. 93–7)

Pyramus and Thisbe as Bottom sees them, the delicate creatures the language allows us to see so clearly, the fantasies of the lovers, horrible or beautiful, come to us with the authority of the plainest prose, even as we are accepting the point that illusions and exaggerations are what humans are fated to treat with as if they were reality. And even when the persons in the play entertain the thought that they are mad, even that the world is mad, it is this very supposition, clung to by all the reasoning they are capable of, that persuades us of the sanity of their portrayal—the persons in this play are not wholly the stuff dreams are made of, this is the dreaming of persons to whom illusion brings real pain.

And if the sense of something not to be accounted for, neither to be expected nor to be prepared for, some ancient fault in the nature of things always somehow giving grounds for fear, the further cause for trepidation is in the sense that is also present that all this that was conceived in the womb of time is the body of fate. During the course of the play the conviction grows that what has happened was fated to, precisely that conviction that gives dreams their special quality of horror, adding to the character that belongs to them of the mysterious and the inexplicable the conviction that we are all powerless before the consequences of ancient causes. This is why it is apposite to recall that the word 'fairies' comes from a word meaning fates, for the supernatural creatures of this play, picturesque and delicate as they are, are as careless and indeflectible as the witches in *Macbeth*.

And at the same time, by the very fancifulness in the invention of these minuscule divinities, the idea that matters are outside our control is being treated playfully. There is fun as well as terror in the idea that fate or fairies or the Olympian gods or nature are all-powerful. All is quiet while Puck goes about his sweeping—there is fun as well as folly in our trusting in his success.

The main goings-on of the play were brought about by the fairies. The matter of ill-matched lovers was there to begin with but without the intrusions of Oberon there would have been no mistaking of Helena by Lysander or of Hermia by Demetrius, nor the straightenings out of the mistakes. That the means of the various enchantments are the works of unseen powers is in one sense inconsequential enough though in another it works together with our understanding that love comes and goes according to no one's plans and that love, too, leads to the mistaking of truth as much as any filter or fiend ever could. The inconsequential and the significant are one, the poetry is the poetry of moonlight where that which is sometimes seems not to be, and that which is not is often most magical. But as the play has it, what happens is the fairies' doing.

The immortals know no morality and they are indifferent to justice. They are very like the Olympian deities except that they are minuscule and hurl only minuscule thunders. But they are similarly proud and splendid, similarly careless, and their interest in mortals is similarly dilettante. Bottom and the mechanicals as the embodiment of common sense comment on the poetry and lunacy of lovers, and the fairies provide their comment on the divinity and misery of lovers and on their subjection to fate. They can comment on the vanity of good sense and prudence and honest labor and on the transience of everything but their own power.

And if Oberon and Titania may be something like the gods, they are also something like the fates, or at least they are as bound up with the errors they have loosed upon the world as the world itself is. They are certainly the determiners of the fortunes of mortals, capriciously transferring affections, righting wrongs at will and as mischievously doing good. But they themselves are as bound up as the mortals they bind, as caught up in the ways of jealousy and recrimination and spite and affection as if those very onsets and attacks and repulsions were the substance of fate itself. What one might think of as the inherently limiting conditions of humans are as compelling and fateful for them.

But there is a strangely ironic twist which gives these particular immortals a character appropriate to beings or powers much greater than even fate, and we may distinguish this from that as the Greeks appear to have done in thinking of ananke, the iron rule of necessity. This is made known to us in the fixity of the relationship of the pair—their union is indissoluble. No matter what the wars they foment in heaven or on earth, what cataclysms and eruptions they cause, they themselves are forever inseparable, they are the very principle of life and union, as fixed in their dependence on each other as any center to a circle.

There is no doubt that in developing the play's action Shakespeare was likening the fairies to the Olympians—Titania accuses Oberon of taking the form of a shepherd in order to make love to Phillida; Oberon accuses Titania of aiding Theseus in his adventures and crimes. The fairy king and his queen are like Zeus and Hera in their everlasting bickering, falling out over some foolish affection of one or the other. They are like what are to be called in *The Winter's Tale* the petty gods. In Homer the sublime often verges on the ridiculous, in this play the ridiculous takes on Elysian loveliness—

> she perforce withholds the lovèd boy,
> Crowns him with flowers, and makes him all her joy.
> And now they never meet in grove or green,
> By fountain clear or spangled starlight sheen,
> But they do square, that all their elves for fear
> Creep into acorn-cups and hide them there.
>
> (II. i. 26–31)

And just as there is irony in the representation of these majestic personages, minuscule and beautiful, so there is in the fury and the wars—the males on the side of Oberon, the females siding with Titania, engaging their forces as seriously as if principle or virtue or justice were at stake, or indeed the governing of the world. And yet for all the vehemence, the rage does not go deep—so Titania says accommodatingly enough to Oberon,

> If you will patiently dance in our round,
> And see our moonlight revels, go with us.
> If not, shun me, and I will spare your haunts.
>
> (II. i. 140–2)

And Oberon's revenge on her lacks the unforgivable malice we know in humans:

I'll watch Titania when she is asleep,
And drop the liquor of it in her eyes.
The next thing then she waking looks upon,
Be it on lion, bear, or wolf, or bull,
On meddling monkey, or on busy ape,
She shall pursue it with the soul of love.
And ere I take this charm from off her sight,
As I can take it with another herb,
I'll make her render up her page to me.

(II. i. 177–85)

Neither Hera nor Zeus knew such mildness.

And in what concerns us more, in the transfers of affection among the mortals, this is not love as we know it in the tragedies, these are true affections certainly, sometimes passive, but mostly charm and intoxication. And so with the vexations, blown up to heroic size, but in fact only a little more serious than falling off a stool or sneezing. The caprices of women, the injuries to a man's pride, the rages of vanity, are endowed with an imaginary magnitude because the infinitesimal creatures at the origin of so much have such apparently tremendous power, which comes down, fundamentally, to the power to delude. But even this the play encourages us to make little of.

What engages us more is the fun in the proposition that humans are as helpless as the creatures in dreams. And in a most important respect—this turning of things inside out, again and again—gods become minims, in their turn behaving like mortals, who from time to time themselves take on like gods—this mockery and irony and playfulness are presented to us with the one qualification that at once explains and excuses all, that this is the way things are in dreams. What brought all this home to us is that from time to time life itself appears to tell us we are powerless to direct our very lives. What will save the persons in the play from the defeats strange powers have contrived for them, and that so enchants us, will be the discovery that it was their powerlessness that was the dream, and that love is something other than enthrallment.

NOTES

[1] This is Coleridge's sense: 'one continued specimen of the lyrical dramatized.' (*Shakespeare Criticism*, in *The Best of Coleridge*, ed. E. L. Griggs, New York, 1934, p. 343).

[2] *The Shakespearian Tempest*, London, 3rd edition, 1953, pp. 328–9.

[3] *Lectures on Shakespeare and Milton*, London, 1883, p. 290.

The Waste of Men

A few years ago a reviewer in *Le Monde* wrote of a stunning performance of *Julius Caesar* in the amphitheater at Lyon.

'At our feet the Senate, the Forum, the luminous realm of columns and pavements where the words, the deeds, the murders themselves one could easily believe were pregnant with the future. And in the air, in the atmosphere, rising above the roofs, above the cypresses, one sensed all that we mean by the fortunes of war, of the revenges of fate, of the vast unfathomable swamps of history which reduce to nothingness the heart's and the mind's desires.

'The *mise en scène* lit up magnificently the duel between light and darkness and between man and what is arrayed against him. Thanks to the stage effects and the lighting which gave the setting the mobility of a great cinema production, the rationalizations of the conspirators showed up in the narrow semi-circle of the stage in all their dubiety. Afterwards, Caesar dead was no different than the carcass of a bird, the crowds a pack of hounds, the quarreling of the conspirators word-music dissolved in the wind.' (Bertrand Poirot-Delpech, June 18, 1964).

No doubt the site of the theater in the center of ancient Gaul was responsible in part for such an evocation but there is an important sense in which the story of an incident in the history of Rome is indeed the subject of Shakespeare's play—it would be a very different work indeed if the events were placed in another scene than the Forum itself, the Capitol and the Campus Martius, placed in ancient Lyon, or Chester, for the play tells of the trembling of the capitol of the world and we draw on all our associations with the name of Rome in attending to it.

It is initially, of course, what all plays are, the representation of persons speaking, engaging each other in business and disputes, working out their interests and needs. And it will continue as all plays do, the persons wrestling with the issues that concern them until there is an end to it. All the same, there hovers over it from the beginning some such sense of vistas as the critic felt in the French theater, vistas of an ancient, tragic, crime-ridden civilization, and the seat of more honor than the western world has known of elsewhere.

The first scene, the first words, show us something of the vitality of the populace and the intensity of the energies at work in the politics of the republic. The turbulent crowd, its stupidities, the anger and sarcasm of the tribunes, are all as it were hurled at us, the eternally famous Roman populace in this evidence of its tempestuous energy bringing before us a sense of the power that is required to lead and govern it. These are the plebeians Antony could tell that Caesar was leaving them his wealth because he loved them. And what in one aspect we take to be revilings and demagogic fraudulence, in another we understand to be signs of the depth of the passions that are kindling murmurs in the offices and shoutings in the streets.

The tribunes, partisans of Pompey, harangue the crowd, blistering them for leaving their work to welcome Caesar on his return to Rome on the feast of Lupercal, threatening them with a plague from the gods for their inconstancy. The next scene, a long one, includes among other matters the account that Caesar has just refused the crown—a kind of trumped-up device of his partisans, we learn from the historians—and now the forebodings of the tribunes, the fears and doubts of Cassius and Brutus, the wild enthusiasms of the people we take to be the precursors of a calamity the heavens themselves announce:

> I have seen tempests, when the scolding winds
> Have rived the knotty oaks, and I have seen
> Th' ambitious ocean swell and rage and foam

To be exalted with the threatn'ing clouds;
But never till tonight, never till now,
Did I go through a tempest dropping fire.
Either there is a civil strife in heaven,
Or else the world, too saucy with the gods,
Incenses them to send destruction. . . .

A common slave (you know him well by sight)
Held up his left hand, which did flame and burn
Like twenty torches joined; and yet his hand,
Not sensible of fire, remained unscorched.

(I. iii. 5–18)

The earth itself 'shook like a thing infirm', and the words tell not only of the anger of the gods but of the threat to Rome in the being and presence of a mere man, Caesar. After the killing itself it is said that the entire open place was suddenly empty, everyone fled, and the body was alone until three slaves came to carry it away. The Roman streets must have been very much like Saint Mark's Square as Tintoretto shows it to us, terror-ridden beneath the storm clouds when the saint's body is being moved. There is this same desolation in Shakespeare's scene when Antony is left alone with the body, to pray and call upon the dogs of war until a servant comes who helps him bear away the corpse.

> You look pale, and gaze,
> And put on fear, and cast yourself in wonder,
> To see the strange impatience of the heavens;
> But if you would consider the true cause
> Why all these fires, why all these gliding ghosts,
> Why birds and beasts, from quality and kind,
> Why old men, fools, and children calculate,
> Why all these things change from their ordinance,
> Their natures and preformed faculties,
> To monstrous quality, why, you shall find
> That heaven hath infused them with these spirits
> To make them instruments of fear and warning
> Unto some monstrous state. (I. iii. 59–71)

Shakespeare brings Caesar on the stage, not as in the triumph itself although with a probably decent train. He seems to have noticed that Caesar had been doing without a bodyguard for some time—this made it possible for the soothsayer to come so close to him—and it is another element in accustoming us to see him apart from the magnificent formality and splendor of his entrance into the city and at the Capitol. After that first appearance with his train, and the first omen, he returns briefly, cast down after the embarrassing events at the Capitol, passing his discomfiture off by speaking rather casually and intimately to Antony of his suspicions of Cassius. He makes no other appearance until the middle of the next act when, in his nightgown, he comes forward while the storm is raging to ask for an interpretation of the dreams that have disturbed his wife whose crying out has roused him. In a most important sense it is he himself who is the cause of the uproar, this man who has appeared so far in the play almost casually, with little fanfare, in undress, presented to us as much as it would be possible to in ordinary circumstance, to whom, we are to understand, the common touch was inherent to his dignity.

> Nor heaven nor earth have been at peace tonight:
> Thrice hath Calphurnia in her sleep cried out,
> 'Help, ho! They murder Caesar!' (II. ii. 1–3)

The representation of him without the furnishings pertaining to grandeur prepares us for the effect he is to have after his death, when, deprived of his very life, a disembodied spirit, he is to dominate the minds of everyone, and, as Brutus is to think of it, must continue to dominate.

That we see as much as we do of Caesar in this light makes us the more impressed by Cassius's characterization of him as the feared Colossus. We have been prepared for the gigantic and monstrous, we know all Rome is at his feet, the wide range of empire is his own creation, and then, seeing him all but removed from ceremony, we are learning the most impressive of all the truths about him, that it is a mere man who has done all this and who demands such awe:

Brutus and Caesar? What should be in that 'Caesar'?
Why should that name be sounded more than yours?
Write them together, yours is as fair a name!
Sound them it doth become the mouth as well;
Weigh them, it is as heavy; conjure with 'em,
'Brutus' will start a spirit as soon as 'Caesar.'
Now, in the names of all the gods at once,
Upon what meat doth this our Caesar feed
That he is grown so great? (I. ii. 142–50)

This is Cassius's point, it is merely a man who is at the bottom of this, and in Cassius's envy and fear there is the other point that is equally essential, the record of Caesar's capacity makes it certain there has never been his equal. He has so enlarged the power of Rome that one could be excused for thinking Nature horrified, the imagination might be warranted that sees streams leaving their banks and rivers flowing backward in the universal terror. The noblest men have necessarily become as fearful of greatness they now discover in their own kind as of the powers in the heavens.

Caesar thinks of himself as incomparable; his conceit, if that is what it is, enlarges him in his own thought beyond any comparison with mortals. And so the likenesses in which he speaks of himself go beyond what even Cassius's envy conjured up about Colossi—

Danger knows full well
That Caesar is more dangerous than he.
We are two lions littered in one day,
And I the elder and more terrible,
And Caesar shall go forth. (II. ii. 44–8)

There goes along with the searching out of inhuman figures the manner of the imperial distance, speaking of himself in the third person, detached, cool, as if removed to Olympus, or as if he were the mountain itself that no Ajax or even Poseidon could budge:

I could be well moved, if I were as you;
If I could pray to move, prayers would move me;
But I am constant as the Northern Star,

Of whose true-fixed and resting quality
There is no fellow in the firmament.
The skies are painted with unnumbered sparks,
They are all fire and every one doth shine;
But there's but one in all doth hold his place.
So in the world: 'tis furnished well with men,
And men are flesh and blood, and apprehensive;
Yet in the number I do know but one
That unassailable holds on his rank,
Unshaked of motion; and that I am he,
Let me a little show it even in this—
That I was constant Cimber should be banished,
And constant do remain to keep him so.

And when Cinna seems to persist in his request—

Hence! Wilt thou lift up Olympus?
(III. i. 58–74)

Antony has this same sense of him after death, ranging among mortals like a spirit hot from hell, or like one of those ancient gods furious in battle—

And Caesar's spirit, ranging for revenge,
With Ate by his side, come hot from hell,
Shall in these confines with a monarch's voice
Cry 'Havoc!' and let slip the dogs of war,
That this foul deed shall smell above the earth
With carrion men, groaning for burial.
(III. i. 270–5)

Cassius earlier had had a like thought;

Now could I, Casca, name to thee a man
Most like this dreadful night,
That thunders, lightens, opens graves, and roars
As doth the lion in the Capitol. (I. iii. 72–5)

Plutarch had given the warrant: this man was indeed leagued with awful powers:

'But his great prosperity and good fortune that favored him all
his lifetime, did continue afterwards in the revenge of his death,
pursuing the murderers both by sea and land, till they had not left
a man more to be executed, of all them that were actors or
counselors in the conspiracy of his death. Furthermore, of all the
chances that happen unto men upon the earth, that which came
to Cassius above all other, is most to be wondered at: for he, being
overcome in battle at the journey of Philippi, slew himself with
the same sword with which he had struck Caesar. Again, of signs
in the element, the great comet, which seven nights together was
seen very bright after Caesar's death, the eighth night after was
never seen more. Also the brightness of the sun was darkened,
that which all that year through rose very pale and shined not out,
whereby it gave but small heat: therefore the air being very
cloudy and dark, by the weakness of the heat that could not come
forth, did cause the earth to bring forth but raw and unripe fruit,
which rotted before it could ripe.'

In short, from the beginning of the play Shakespeare is moving
towards the most awesome effects of tragedy through partly
ironic means. He uses images of the familiar and the slight to
establish the sense of the great and the horrible and the celestial.
He communicates the sense of supreme greatness in representing
the assurance that was once found in a man among men.

A writer who regarded all that his imagination worked on
with the most searching intellectual concern could not but
approach a subject from ancient history with more than an
interest in the representation of artifacts. In adapting an ancient
comedy Shakespeare had informed a story about separated twins
with romantic and Christian meanings. In dramatizing the
history of his own people he had drawn on religious and philosophic doctrines. He would have been out of character, in taking
over a subject from pagan antiquity, if he had not represented
ancient meanings in the light of his own dispensation. And when,
in *Julius Caesar*, we see him giving the most brilliant expression
to all sorts of beliefs and superstititions, we very quickly

understand that in the integrity of such a re-creation there is as exacting a scrutiny as we find in Montaigne.

It is accordingly all the more helpful to have the testimony of one of the most distinguished historians of ancient Rome that Shakespeare's reconstruction of the life of the times in this play is so faithful, so free from distortion, that, as he put it, historians must despair of their own attempts to evoke the actuality. I should like to quote from Professor Jérome Carcopino at some length, partly in gratitude for the character of his appreciation of Shakespeare's accomplishment, but partly, too, in order to prepare for a consideration of what more Shakespeare was in fact accomplishing.

'I very much fear that a historian who had the good fortune to be present at Barrault's impressive production of Shakespeare's *Julius Caesar*, leaving the theater, could not but become melancholy, accusing himself, as a historian, of wasting his time and trouble, laboring day after day over documents there is never an end to searching out, dissecting texts, weighing evidence, at first hastily, and then examining it from every side, while this poet, with a single fleeting glance, got at the essential truths the historian only gropes after, which he could only hesitantly flatter himself he had got at after lengthy analysis and at the cost of great effort.

'Far from falsifying reality, Shakespeare has rendered it truly, not only to our intelligence but to our feelings. With an astonishing sureness of touch he has taken anecdotes from his reading, and, giving them a certain magnitude in the verse, he has used them to unravel a story through devices of suspense that reveal the very path of fate. . . .

'Shakespeare's perspicacity is so rich and acute that professional historians can only ask whether he does not indeed have second sight. . . . In the play Cicero plays but a minor part, but in the few exchanges he appears in his authentic visage. . . . No historian knows any better than Shakespeare how to guide us in following the meanderings of Brutus's soul, at once virtuous and criminal, scrupulously cynical, and endlessly tormented by doubts and remorse. . . .'[1]

Helped by such a testimonial to maintain the normal supposition that Shakespeare intended to achieve an effect of authenticity, we nevertheless observe that much else has gone into the forming of the play. We recognize along with the faithful absorptions of the material in Plutarch and Appian some falsifications that served the needs of drama as such. The Lupercalia, themselves in February, are supposed to have taken place at about the time of the assassination, in mid-March. Caesar's triumph over Pompey's sons, which had taken place in the preceding October, is here supposed to have occurred just previous to the feast of the Lupercalia in February, when Caesar refused the crown. Supernatural portents, occurring over a period of time, are similarly crowded together. There are other telescopings, as there are important omissions, particularly matters involving the strife between Antony and Octavius. It is clear that all this is effected in order that we shall be as little distracted as possible from the main action, the progress of the plot against Caesar and the major events leading to the deaths of Cassius and Brutus. The point should be made, however, that the tamperings introduce nothing that falsifies what is being accurately transcribed.

Accurately transcribed from his sources, and however little Shakespeare took from Appian, however much from Plutarch, we would not need the testimony of Professor Carcopino to remind us that Shakespeare was not treating merely with written records. He was treating with the life they spoke of, the turbulent Rome at the time of the Republic's death, and of men coping with issues on which their lives depended and on which, in other forms, in other times, other lives were to depend. The question now becomes, as one imagines a production of the play, on seeing Caesar with his entourage and hearing of the race of the naked men, assisting at the funeral, what is it we are to imagine, a re-creation of the scenes of Plutarch, or of the scenes themselves? Not that Shakespeare would have had any way of knowing all we can know about the way a great Roman funeral was managed, or that he could have divined very much that Appian himself did not know about Antony's conduct and his actual speech. Or that Shakespeare would have had a just appreciation of all that was involved in the talk about the deification of a man. But Professor Carcopino's remarks assure us of what we did not need his authority for, that Shakespeare was doing better than Plutarch and Appian, doing better than any account that ever was or ever could have been, his imagination was peopling the scene as only his could have, and as near as may be as reality itself, if it could speak, would certify.

The claim is not absurd.[2] It is rich and strange, of course, and it calls upon our faith. And it is therefore interesting, and, I believe, rewarding, to put beside a couple of Shakespeare's scenes the fuller accounts modern historians can provide of some of these matters, providing details we may borrow to fill out Shakespeare's scenes only to discover how little they modify his representation.

For example, it is good to know with assurance how vast the historic Caesar's ambitions were, what was truly signified by the cult of his divinization, for when in total ignorance we reflect upon Cassius's suspicions in the play about Caesar's motives we may not credit them with the seriousness they deserve. Similarly, we may take Brutus's slowness in responding to the threat of Caesar's tyranny as an index of a character generally slow to act, and we may not think to refer his silence to the fact that the danger had been obvious to Brutus for a long time and the question for him had become not simply—should we act now? but this, too, is it not already too late?

'It was probably on his Eastern campaigns that Caesar conceived the plan of a Roman version of the ruler cult. There it was a political and religious necessity to claim for himself what had been due to the kings of the East; Dea Roma as a religious bond no longer sufficed to hold the parts of his empire together. In Rome itself his new position was to be prepared in the Roman fashion by the honours mentioned above. In the past the gods had represented a continuity, a never-changing authority, in contrast to that of the annual magistrates. Now their authority was to be shared by Caesar, who therefore required religious backing. These preparations were intensified when the Parthian campaign became imminent. In Parthia Caesar meant to appear as a legitimate king, the heir to all its political and religious traditions, and he wished to be honoured accordingly. It may well be that he drove into Rome in his triumph of 46 in a chariot with white horses precisely because that was how the Persian kings used to appear. Later he wore, or planned to wear, the Eastern tunic and wanted to wear the diadem. [The coronets on the statues in Shakespeare's play and the crown he refused three times were diadems of the Persian style.] In Rome his house received a pediment; he wore the shoes of the Alban kings and rode like a king into Rome on horseback. His cult was decreed and a priest-hood created. During his long absence his cult was to become established in Rome and Italy and perhaps to prepare for more. The Parthian victory would have consolidated his empire in the East, and the West would have followed suit.'[3]

The man who had lately left Cleopatra in Egypt with a son, who was moved to surpass the splendor of the Magi, would be entering the scenes of Shakespeare's play with such a sense of grandeur that Cassius's comparison with the Colossus could seem beggarly. The fears of Shakespeare's Cassius we learn we must measure against what is truly appalling, the ways of the gods, and a man who does indeed seem to have something of their power and something of their manner. We are less disposed, accordingly, to cut Cassius down to the size of a merely envious man. No one was ever more portentous than the man he feared.

Then there is the funeral.

As the editors point out, Shakespeare gives us some indication that he was attending to certain details in the ancient accounts, for example, that Brutus was speaking in the Forum before the body had been brought into the open on its bier. There is the reference to the procession in which it was carried to the house afterwards, and there are the remarks of the plebeians that indicate they are now to be permitted to crown the statues with the coronets the tribunes had forced them to remove in the first of the play. Shakespeare also follows the source in having Antony ascend the public rostrum to make his speech over the body itself, and afterwards having him descend to the side of the hearse when he points to the wounds in the body. And when the plebeians cry—

> *First Plebeian.* O piteous spectacle!
> *Second Plebeian.* O noble Caesar!
> *Third Plebeian.* O woeful day!
> *Fourth Plebeian.* O traitors, villains!
> *First Plebeian.* O most bloody sight!
> *Second Plebeian.* We will be revenged.—
>
> (III. ii. 197–202)

this may very well be, as it has been suggested, that they are performing as the mourners of the formal chorus did in the ancient ceremony. A production of the play, in Shakespeare's time and now, would properly draw on an account of the ways so many of these things did in fact take place, for an unhistoric improvisation might very well lose touch with Shakespeare's view of the events:

'The preparations included the setting up of a shrine on the Rostra and of the funeral pyre on the Campus Martius next to the tomb of Iulia. The heralds who announced the funeral directed the public to come and bring their gifts by all routes possible to the Campus Martius, that is, not to join the funeral cortège: the precedent of Sulla clearly showed that it would have been an endless procession. The cortège proper began at the house, the *domus publica* at the Regia, with the usual participants, musicians, dancers, *mimi*, and *imagines*, followed by the exhibits. Torch-bearers and freedmen whom Caesar had just set free by testament preceded the couch, on which normally the corpse was lying or reclining; this time it was hidden inside and represented outside by an image in wax. The couch—which was of ivory with coverlets of gold and purple—was carried by the magistrates and ex-magistrates and not as at a private funeral by members of the family. These followed with the rest of the dignitaries and the people. When the Forum was reached gladiatorial contests were held. At the Rostra the ivory couch was placed in the gilded shrine which had been made on the model of the temple of Venus

Genetrix and erected there, and Caesar's robe was hung on a pole which was somehow attached to the shrine.'[4]

This is what Appian says of Antony's conduct:

'Piso brought forth *Cæsars* body, to the which, infinit numbers in armes ran, to kepe it, and with much noyse and pompe, brought it to the place of speech. There was much lamentation and weeping, ther was rushing of harnesse togither, with repentaunce of the forgetting of reuengeance. *Antony* marking how they were affected, did not let it slippe, but toke vpon him to make *Cæsars* funeral sermon, as Consul, of a Consul, friend, of a friend, and kinsman, of a kinsman (for *Antony* was partly his kinsman) and to/vse craft againe. And thus he said:

'"I do not thinke it meete (O Citizens) that the buriall praise of suche a man, should rather be done by me, than by the whole country. For what you haue altogither for the loue of hys vertue giuen him by decree, aswell the Senate as the people, I thinke your voice, and not *Antonies*, oughte to expresse it."

'This he vttered with sad and heauy cheare, and wyth a framed voice, declared euery thing, chiefly vpon the decree, whereby he was made a God, holy and inuiolate, father of the country, benefactor and gouernor, and suche a one, as neuer in al things they entituled other man to the like. At euery of these words *Antonie* directed his countenance and hands to *Cæsars* body, and with vehemencie of words opened the fact. At euery title he gaue an addition, with briefe speach, mixte with pitie and indignation. And when the decree named him father of the Country, then he saide: *This is the testimony of our duety*.'[5]

And at the conclusion the people as a choir utter their lamentations:

'And when he had made these and many other inuocations, he tourned hys voice from triumphe to mourning matter, and began to lament and mone him as a friend that had bin vniustly vsed, and did desire that he might guie hys soule for *Cæsars*. Then falling into most vehement affections, vncouered *Cæsars* body, holding up his vesture with a speare, cut with the woundes, and redde with the bloude of the chiefe Ruler, by the which the people lyke a Quire, did sing lamentation vnto him, and by this passion were againe replete with ire. And after these speeches, other lamentations wyth voice after the Country custome, were sung of the Quires, and they rehearsed again his acts and his hap.'[6]

On one of the key matters we must be sure we are not reading into the conflict between Brutus and Caesar the conflict between republicanism and tyranny with the emphasis that belongs to our times, and equally we must not suppose Shakespeare was translating the ancient conflict into a reading of contemporary political matters. On subordinate issues as well it is important to get the right bearings. For instance, in the first scene, the tribunes Marullus and Flavius rebuke the artisans for backing off from their adulation of Pompey, running to bow before the conqueror of Pompey's sons. I believe we are not to take this as simply a slur at the traditionally fickle character of the masses. While the play does not give a full view of the complexity of opinion in Rome, there is nothing, on the other hand, to warrant so simplified a representation. Professor Kittredge long ago warned against imposing any partisan interpretation on the play, most especially rejecting the idea that its drift was governed either by monarchical or republican sympathies, and this argues against too close an identification of the plebeians with a mob. How Shakespeare represented the happenings following the assassination makes this clear, for it is a cause that is disintegrating, conspirators are falling out and the struggle for power becomes known for what it is, a struggle between warlords. Shakespeare evidently chose to present this as a very complex matter, and however much the play brings before us the idea of the supernatural and the possibility of supernatural agency—whether as fate or destiny or retributive justice—he gives us the most vivid sense of the extent of the mere mess. The modern historian's account squares almost too well with the way the play ends.

'For the remainder of the Republic the issues on which there was division in politics were no longer deep questions of principle, as with the Gracchi and the younger Drusus they had been. The severe republicanism of Cato, the pleadings for orderly and balanced government made by Cicero in his speeches and writings and the idealism of M. Brutus were not the determining forces of history. Instead events moved in the direction to which Marius' reforms and Sulla's career had pointed; towards the conflict of great army commanders and the personal rule of the ultimate victor. The restored power of the tribunes was chiefly exercised in the interests of the great generals.'[7]

And so, too, when at the beginning we see Shakespeare's Julius Caesar enter the scene, when we observe the hurly-burly, the concentration on the moments immediately preceding the explosion, the bringing to birth of the monstrous act, we remind ourselves that this was indeed a fatal moment in a long series of moments. The ferocious criticism focussed on the entrances and exits of this great man had been made for years. There had gone into their making not only the respect due the marvelous character and energy of the great conqueror, all that the world endowed him with of its admiration and understanding, there was the sense of time's passing, of the decades in which the governments of Rome and the provinces had been teetering between the authority of the Senate and the ambitions of the generals on whom Rome's greatness depended.

Caesar's reputation made it possible for Shakespeare to present him briefly and in bold strokes, and while in these few scenes the characterization gives us a fine sense of his presence we have agreed in advance, so to speak, to credit what his admirers as well as his detractors say of him. It is Cassius who introduces the idea of the Colossus but Caesar himself was to outdo that with the analogy to Olympus. Yet if in this play Caesar were going by another name I think an audience would have hardly more sense of him than as an overblown fear. With the name he does bear he brings with him the idea and the air of one of the greatest of all men and in the representation of his assassination we know we are being told of one of the critical events of our civilization.

We do not need to be well-read to get this meaning for the

issues bearing upon liberty and tyranny are always of the greatest consequence, and the theme would magnify the acts of even small men. But as important a means as any leading into a sense of the magnitude of the action is the air of factuality Shakespeare gives to supernatural matters. By the circumstantiality and vividness with which these are brought before us Shakespeare more than makes up for the ignorance of history of the most uninstructed audience. He appeals on the one hand to the incidents the ancient records have related in precise detail, and on the other to the fears and doubts of any audience when told of violent disturbances as if they had indeed taken place, in the skies and under ground, at the very time the state was troubled. Even sceptics at the time could not but take notice as they observed the effects of the panic upon the sober. Cassius may have bared his breast to the lightning but the defiance itself acknowledged enough, and later, of course, when the going got very rough he was less bold. At the beginning, prophetically, describing the terror the very thought of Caesar excited in him, Cassius likened the dictator to just such violent motions as were to be seen now upsetting heaven and earth:

> Now could I, Casca, name to thee a man
> Most like this dreadful night
> That thunders, lightens, opens graves, and roars
> As doth the lion in the Capitol. (I. iii. 72–5)

Bodies in flame, spirits gibbering, the earth convulsed, the language that describes this with all the vividness of factuality attests to the quality of a man whose downfall these disturbances announce, and that will bring others even more ruinous upon the city and the world.

This is as Cassius sees it, who will risk everything rather than endure a greater horror. And the audience, with whatever knowledge of history it has and with whatever sense of actuality the play establishes, is led to share in his awe and fear. And there is still more to move us than even Cassius articulates as we learn that these awful powers in the heavens, signalling their displeasure, will yet do nothing to prevent the murder.

Yet even while we are being impressed with the magnitude of these men and of the issues in the very world of fact, the play is also working to the opposite sense, to the revelation of their pettiness, of their folly and superstition, and to an understanding of the action itself as mere politics. The last words of the play are from Octavius, of all men the least brilliant and the least feeling—

> So call the field to rest, and let's away
> To part the glories of this happy day—

a heavenly and an infernal drama has been played out and he calls it 'this happy day'! We allow ourselves to appreciate the point of view even while it brings into contempt all the concern we have been feeling. Yet what it alludes to is the way it was: Caesar and Antony made up a party. They were to seize power and govern Rome. A faction rose to oppose them, and killed Caesar. At the very moment of their success Antony turned the tables on them, brought Octavius on the scene and came out on top.[8] Brilliant enough, of course, and the passion on Antony's part fascinating, but, all together, squalid and criminal. The smaller men won out. Those who opposed the Colossus—Cassius and Brutus—were themselves giants compared to the wastrel and the schemer who were to overcome them. If they were not, in Cassius' word, pygmies, they were certainly lesser and luckier men. The whole action, in short, was just another power play.

All along, in fact, we were being given to understand that what to some is grand beyond all conception, to others is mean, that the drama some think they are playing out on the great stage of civilization is to others a cynical performance, just as we in the audience are free to take the talk about disturbances among the celestial and infernal powers as so much nonsense.

In short, all this that has to do with greatness and with the divine, with affairs of state and ceremonies and apparitions, is at one and the same time a playing with belief and with disbelief. At the very moment we are absorbed in the thought of greatness it is being mocked. We are asked to think at once reverently and sardonically of divine powers concerning themselves with human affairs. The stress on what is petty in the motivations of men emphasizes the magnitude of their pretensions. The uproar combined with the magnificence both terrifies and enthralls.

The techniques of irony are so various and so pervasive that one may conclude that diminution quite as much as magnification is creating the impression of grandeur. The womanish vanity of Caesar, the mean-spirited envy of Cassius, the hysterical strain in Brutus where he seems to be alluding to the scandalous rumor that Caesar was his father—

> Our reasons are so full of good regard,
> That were you, Antony, the son of Caesar
> You should be satisfied—
>
> (III. i. 224–6)

all these signs of frailness, like the sight of Caesar in nightdress do not diminish but accentuate the nobility and the horror. Empire and glory and principle are at the beck and call of creatures old wives gabble about and in the very grotesqueness the wonder of it all is enhanced.

The irony turns upon itself. All that is so plainly trivial and false calls into question not only our belief but our disbelief in greatness. All these toyings with truth lead us as they do in *A Midsummer Night's Dream* to the thought of matters of great constancy. It is not in establishing a two-fold vision through the contrast of the great and the small that Shakespeare achieves the grandest effects of tragedy, but through a single vision in which great and small are shown to be the same, actuality and aspiration as projections of each other, the merely human as also the transcendently important.

And so as the play moves to its end one wave-like motion, as Professor H. T. Price once spoke of it, is succeeded by another. The great enterprise of saving the republic was thwarted by the adherents to the fallen hero, civil war followed, confederates fell out, battles ended in suicides, and the end was a fluky victory and a fatuous epitaph. In this enactment of a decline from greatness, if I may summarize the action so, the audience is raised to a state of the noblest awe, to a sense of nobility and royalty that is within the range of only the greatest tragedies. We see before us the greatest and the noblest the world has known reduced to pieces of bleeding earth and in the sight of that wasting we experience the exaltation of those who have known greatness and the unearthly.

The indications the play gives of the importance of destiny are quite ambiguous, and in the complexity with which now this, now that conclusion is pointed to, we are being entertained with ironies that match those brought forward by the nature of the action.

The play moves regularly and swiftly. There is a primary motion in which a faction forms to seize power and as it succeeds engenders a counter-movement, losing its own momentum as that of its enemies grows. The original action commenced as a party of Senators determined that Caesar's ambitions were a threat to the constitution of Rome. The issue was defined by fears of what might be rather than by the knowledge of what was, and as a consequence the entire enterprise, in policy and in execution, rested on un-certainties. The ambitions of Caesar to some extent, his aims even more, and more still the consequences of his removal were never all that clear. The good sought for by the conspirators was as uncertainly defined as the evil feared, but the conviction grew that the stakes were of supreme importance. It seemed, also, that other than human powers were involved. There is no one who can completely gainsay the witnesses of apparitions and the play treats the belief in divinity too sympathetically and profoundly to allow us to refer it all to superstition. Too many strange occurrences have been noted for us to dispose of them all equally as of no consequence. What is of more importance to us than the status of the supernatural is the mysteriousness, the enigmatic import of the signs. That things are being brought to birth is certain; that troubles are ahead; that there is much that cannot be forestalled; that the future does announce itself, and that there are indeed signs: all this we are never able to deny, but what is and what is not a sign, and what a sign imports, about that we are never to be satisfied. The play, for its part, insists on the mysterious, on the enigmatic. The signs, the warnings, all that speaks of fate, is kept before us so continuously that we are always being compelled to discover if the sense of supernatural agency is indeed giving us a light to see by. But what above all else directs us to accept the drama as one played out in the sight of the gods is the character and depth of Caesar's faith, uncertain in treating with particular manifestations and interventions but unclouded in essential conviction.

He believes himself to be a man of destiny and, as such, a creature and a fellow of the gods. His magnificent words in one sense signify the composure of the courageous and in another they express the serenity of the perfectly faithful—

> What can be avoided
> Whose end is purposed by the mighty gods? . . .
> Cowards die many times before their deaths;
> The valiant never taste of death but once.
> Of all the wonders that I yet have heard,
> It seems to me most strange that men should fear,
> Seeing that death, a necessary end,
> Will come when it will come.
>
> (II. ii. 26–7, 32–7)

Whatever the dominant thought, the words in every sense are beautiful and noble, and not least for the note of reverence.

In these words as in much else we are given the notion of the events of life running their course. The underlying figure in the imagining is that of a river—not of a web with a pattern, a design that can be grasped as it were by the sight, but of a movement in time, obeying laws no doubt, but in accord with patterns we cannot visualize as we think we can when we speak of design. Whatever its basis the conviction is certain. The same way of thinking is Brutus's—

> There is a tide in the affairs of men
> Which, taken at the flood, leads on to fortune;

Omitted, all the voyage of their life
Is bound in shallows and in miseries.
On such a full sea are we now afloat,
And we must take the current when it serves
Or lose our ventures. (IV. iii. 218–24)

With such a view of the ways of the universe men do not so much
seek to propitiate as to consult in order to learn how to exercise
their freedom. They are confident that the universe permits, is
even at times solicitous of their flourishing. It is governed by laws,
and the acts of men may join in harmony with them. It is only
required that men be bold and upright. The belief is inexpugnable,
however enigmatic the patterns of circumstance and the appearance of signs. It is enough to understand that in this accord there
is the ground for belief in providential care.

Antony's mockery—

Fortune is merry
And in this mood will give us anything—
(III. ii. 271–2)

affirms what it is playfully pointing to, the indefinable principle
governing the flow of rivers, the course of time, the opportunities
of men. He does not mean that a capricious all-ruling power is
emptying her bag of gifts, but rather that that which has gifts in
its power is giving them abundantly at this particular time for
those who put out their hands. The name of Fortune is apposite
not because the universe is lawless but because it is inscrutable.

There is a tide, the universe is ordered, and all that leads men
to agree also leads them at times to suppose that the ordering of
things has something to do with justice. Shakespeare follows the
contemporary, not the ancient, suggestion that the spirit that
appeared to Brutus at Philippi was Caesar's, and this of course
suggests a retributive spirit working through non-human powers.
The sword with which Cassius struck Caesar he and Titinius used
to kill themselves. Then, too, man after man comes to his downfall
through some apparently ineradicable trait of his nature—as

Brutus puts it—'nature must obey necessity.' (IV. iii. 227) Brutus's own idealism, Caesar's vanity, Cassius's defective eyesight, may have made their downfall inevitable. And then, too, there is the sense the audience must make much of, that since it is history we are attending to all will take place according to its known end.[9]

Yet when we make all of this that we feel we must, we are still enthralled by the belief that the play in its very crisis is representing, that men are right to cherish their freedom. The idea of free will that Brutus and Cassius are honoring and that Caesar in his own way magnifies obtains our subscription quite as fully as does the idea of the ineluctable. No matter what is to be said about the limitations of the character of these men no one in the play is so plainly the prisoner of his nature as Macbeth or even Bottom.

I think that in the end one may conclude no more about what is surely fated than every one admits to, and that Brutus puts well enough—

> That we shall die, we know; 'tis but the time,
> And drawing days out, that men stand upon.
>
> (III. i. 99–100)

Tribonius has just used the word 'Doomsday', which seems to stand for the ancient *fatalis dies*, the day of death, and to say no more than that. But it does indicate that the course of history following the fall of Caesar is what we know it to be, little more than a record of the crimes and follies of mankind, where many lives will be nasty, brutish, and short, and where Rome will have fallen. But in the play there is no suggestion that hindsight any more than foresight could plot the course that led necessarily to that end.

A central consideration to the maintenance of this conclusion is the evidently indelible conviction of the fact of human greatness, of the power and dignity that inheres in the choices men make. It is the independence, of Caesar's above all others', that asserts this. From one point of view one may say the final testimony is that which Pierre Boyancé has asserted of the historic matter, that Caesar's spirit is still seeking revenge after twenty centuries. He

embodies—what? greatness? divinity? power?—that will never
be subdued. The final reverence of Brutus for him as he dies
witnesses his lasting ascendancy in the world of the play as it may
sustain the reputation of the historic figure.

The final irony is not that fate is indefinable and unintelligible
but that it is intractable, and that power is intractable, and it is
power that men are unable to manage. Reason can no more grasp
its nature than it can grasp the nature of fate. It is reasonless. And
if one were to suppose that the play gives us such paradoxes as that
power is law and law is fate and power is fate, the conclusion would
be that no meaning is to be fathomed to the relationships between
humans and the world. When Brutus says to the spirit—

O Julius Caesar, thou are mighty yet!—
(V. iii. 94)

he is saying not only that principle and purpose and justice, as men
define them and would grant them their allegiance, are inadequate
to rule even the affairs of men, he is saying that in the face of things
as they are men are intrinsically obtuse, ignorant of the occasions
that are calling forth their efforts. The appeal to righteousness as
the appeal to truth and to tradition are but paltry motions to
control the flood. The point of Caesar's success, as long as it lasted,
was that while worship is required, no man knows well enough the
code he must follow. It may be true that, as Caesar says, he is
unassailable, but in the end he does not know any better than we
what that means.

The world that is host to this greatness and is itself so vast looks
down upon Colossus and pygmy alike. The portents in the heavens
that point implacably to the overthrow of the great man are as
careless of the man who works untiringly to destroy him. Cassius
is incapable of giving up, all his strength and intelligence and
devotion he commits to the single task, yet the world has as little
care for that perfection of his, that humanity and skill and decency
as it has for Caesar's greatness. It does not even care to choose him
for its own, to lay hands upon him, it cares least of all to regard
him as a power and an agency for superintendent powers. The

world lowering over Rome gives no evidence of designs for either the mighty or the weak, it appears to have no use for any mortal, it takes no part in their upheavals, it only allows itself to be known as the ultimate terror. It is not simply that petty men walk like ants beneath the Colossi, the petty and the great are like minuscule atomies beneath the turbulence of the overarching skies.

The irony again is that after the assassination there is no one to take the tide at the full, energy flags, the enemy turns out to be hydra-headed. The friends fall out, and in falling out become dearer to us than ever, mere goodness peeping out from the confusion, mere goodness the only consequence of their awful try at greatness, their effort to out-match the mightiest. So that the heavens, looking upon better men than it once shone on and then frowned on and left dangling, as Brutus and Cassius compose their differences in love, do not descend, to tell us that the greatest days of Rome are yet to come, that Augustus will set the seal on the greatest achievement of mankind. They simply look down upon a world where truth and love and goodness and magnificence are squandered.

So that the play ends with something of the awe and serenity we have learned to ask of tragedy, ourselves more intent upon greatness than pettiness, more upon awful and divine matters than upon the trivial and inconsequential. And as much as anything this is due to what one might believe the least to be expected factor of all, the representation of beauty in the men who have brought down greatness. The very ones who were unworthy, who at the crisis were found lacking, came to shine in their innate excellence more than in the time before their spoiling. By this we come to respect and tolerate the Sphinx-like reticence of the heavenly powers that stirred such a pother over the city—the marvellous nobility of Cassius and Brutus has about it the integrity of beauty.

The quarrel of Brutus and Cassius is quick with the passion not merely of comrades in arms but of fellows clinging together in continuing to oppose the greatest of catastrophes, in continuing, even, to oppose the gods. The love of Portia, the tenderness of Brutus towards the sleeping boy—

Gentle knave, good night—
(IV. iii. 269)

the gratuitous splendor in the words preparing for the death of
Titinius—

Mistrust of my success hath done this deed—
(V. iii. 65)

is the final, most memorable chime in the splendid music. Shakespeare has been lavish in ennobling with beauty the death of one
after another. In the midst of the final butchery, so differently
than in *Hamlet*, there is the note of splendor.

NOTES

[1] *Rencontres de l'Histoire et de la Littérature Romaines*, Paris, 1963, pp. 271–4.

[2] Mr. Emrys Jones has made this point as part of his sustained analysis of
the structure of the play: 'there is not the slightest pretence that what we
are watching is anything other than an evocation of historical realities'.
(*Scenic Form in Shakespeare*, Oxford, 1971, p. 45).

[3] Stephan Weinstock, *Divus Julius*, Oxford, 1970, pp. 350–1.

[4] *Ibid.*, p. 413.

[5] *Shakespeare's Appian*, edited by Ernest Schanzer, Liverpool, 1956, p. 42.

[6] *Ibid.*, pp. 44.

[7] J. P. V. D. Balsdon, 'The Revolution and the End of Freedom', *The
Romans*, ed. J. P. V. D. Balsdon, New York, 1965, p. 40.

[8] Mr. R. A. Foakes has put this somewhat tentatively: 'various themes . . .
perhaps indicate that the structural unity of *Julius Caesar* lies in the birth
and the completion of the rebellion. . . . this view of the play as being
about faction, and the waste and destruction that attends it'. ('An
Approach to *Julius Caesar*', *Shakespeare Quarterly*, V [1954], 263).

[9] I am in accord with the way in which Mr. J. M. R. Margeson has put the matter in a chapter headed 'A Realm between Faith and Doubt': '. . . there is behind all this some sense of destiny that is not merely the moral law of an intelligible universe. Caesar's murder is fated, as dream and prophecy and the sympathetic distress of nature reveal. Shakespeare makes no attempt to narrow down the causes to one explanation, but allows each to stand as a possible interpretation—retribution, necessity, and fortune—even though retribution in the form of revenge is the most powerful.' (*The Origins of English Tragedy*, Oxford, 1972, p. 160).

The Undiscovered Country

I

In antiquity the presence of the altar in the orchestra of the theater added meaning to the mention of the gods in the drama enacted beside it. In the Renaissance, even when the gods take visible form, we are obliged to think of them as phantasms or as metaphorical representations. Christian deity does not appear, of course, although angels and devils may, yet while sacred matters are brought forward through a variety of means they could not be presented with the authority the stage itself would confer when it held the sacrificial table of a living cult. However sympathetically these later audiences respond to oaths and prayers and apparitions, the commitment to belief is necessarily restrained. Most often, of course, when Renaissance playwrights mention or represent the deities of the ancients they are merely inviting us to reflect upon such likeness as they have to our own gods, or, rather more often, they seem to ask us simply to think of other than human powers as it were at large in the universe. Related to the concerns of humans the ancient names encourage our disposition to awe, but however much we are drawn to think of them as beings and potencies we are not able to pay them the respect the persons in the dramas pay them. We must, for example, strain to respond with anything like the feelings of Orestes in honoring the obligations the gods have set him.

Lear's Apollo, Macbeth's witches, Antony's Hercules have little more than the character of the beings summoned by Prospero from earth and sky. The audience does not believe them authentic although we will allow them to testify to a spirit world we may be persuaded to credit. They exploit our sense of the generically divine and as such they hold our attention as long as some offensive falseness does not distract us. We are willing to accept them as powers residing in a realm outside that known to our senses, coming out of nowhere as we may think the fury has that overpowered Leontes, or that dim premonition of his glory ready to flame forth in Macbeth. But we are put off when the features of Olympus or Hell or Hades become so vivid they suggest not only superstition but artifice, and so invite disbelief and ridicule.

Even in *Hamlet* when we are led to picture a place beyond the reach of the living, the drift of what we are told keeps us from imagining the particulars of Hell or Purgatory. In the pain the dead are said to suffer we recognize the same pain living persons know, and this in itself is enough to provoke the thought of lasting punishment since pain by its very character carries the threat of the interminable. But what it is that would be punishing, and how it would be functioning as punishment, we cannot know even when we are told divinity has arranged a system of rewards and penalties. Even what is offered as revelation may be a lie. Yet if we concur at all with what Hamlet means when he says that every man deserves a whipping, that something—whatever we name it— has been defiled, our ignorance of who or what it is that set the penalty may even intensify our wonder and awe. I do not suppose we can measure the difference between such a sense and that the ancients knew in referring the action before them to the religion to which the altar belonged upon which sacrifice was offered. But for them, we suppose, as well as for moderns the fear of the unknown would inhere in the belief.

For all that Shakespeare's plays suggest of the working of destiny and providence, remote sometimes, it appears, sometimes all-determining, they rarely encourage us to think of them as powers having the form of persons. Ariel, addressing the men of sin, suggests an authoritative deity, but the minister himself being fantastic any image we may commence to form of the deity quickly dissolves. Everything goes to convince us of activities of incalculable power, but the names as much as the habitations of the gods are always ready to vanish into air.

Professor Merchant speaks of those early words of Marcellus as the most vivid reference in all Shakespeare to the Incarnation—

> Some say that ever, 'gainst that season comes
> Wherein our Saviour's birth is celebrated,
> The bird of dawning singeth all night long.
>   (I. i. 158–60)[1]

But what these words point to is nowhere in the play allowed to call for such an utterance and such definite picturing as Aeschylus requires of the Suppliants—

> Zeus, great Saviour of pure homes,
>   Worshipped third when wine is poured,—
> Kindly entrance 'neath yon domes
>   May ye one and all afford. (Campbell)

Prospero said that it is the actual that is evanescent, the physical and the concrete, and Hamlet conceives that this may also be the case of all that indicates direction and purpose in the agencies revealing themselves through the Ghost and in the stirrings within his thoughts. This is the manner of Shakespeare almost everywhere. The ambassadors to Delphos may report of the celestial habits of the priestesses, of the air of sanctity, of the sense of the annihilation of the self in their presence, but the particularity goes no farther. What the god and his dwelling-place were like there is no one to say. In still another heaven-like place it is imagined that souls may couch on flowers, but the paradox distracts us with an image we are not quite able to accommodate. We are in fact given what we most require, the indeterminate. And we find ourselves being confirmed in the suspicion that like the image itself, and the great globe itself, the sense of such powers, enthralling as it is, could be of our own conjuring. The splendor of the idea of providence, the marvellous care alluded to in the language of the New Testament—of the fall of the sparrow—like the fear of the implacable and the remorseless, all make themselves known to us only intermittently, like truth and reality themselves not certainly within our knowledge.

Yet the plays are always proposing that divinity whether directed or blind, is to be known as a constant and an effectual power. In some the protagonists are impelled to decipher its workings, driven earnestly or even desperately to discover its instruments and its purposes. So it is with Caesar and Hamlet and Lear, and they also look for guidance. With Prospero it goes farther than this for he is determined to join in an alliance with the divine. Yet all will share the sense of so many in *A Midsummer Night's Dream*, that they are powerless, and that what they take to be actuality may be a dream. Sensing themselves to be enchanted or enthralled, they still entertain the thought they may not be. By the fact that they are able to conceive of life as illusion they show they retain the idea of what it means to be free. Whether it be Hermia or Ferdinand or Antipholus of Syracuse, the thought of being freed from the dream measures the compass and limits of all constraints, referring even ideas about destiny and providence to thought as itself able to conceive of the limitless.

Hamlet thinks in just such terms, and what is pecularly important to the forming of the play is the identification of his explorings with those of the dramatist himself. Shakespeare's sympathy with Hamlet is so close we come to identify the burden and the resolution of the action with the progress of Hamlet's own reasonings. One may in this matter accept Taine's 'Hamlet is Shakespeare'. In the other plays we easily distinguish between the author's meanings and the expressions of those he allows to seem to speak for him—Berowne, Bottom, Prospero. But no one of these has hardly struck the note we may think of as Shakespeare's own before in that joy he takes in giving individuality its full play the dramatist returns them to themselves. Yet I think one may say that for all Hamlet's idiosyncrasies the author's sympathy with him is perfect, and through the entire action we feel that the protagonist is looking at the world in essentials in no other way than his author. We take the thought as Shakespeare's because we cannot conceive of any greater analytical or metaphorical power in the author than we conceive in this creature of his. Each merges in the other as we see the one manipulating a plot, the other guiding his manipulations.

Hamlet must discover what authority he is to grant the Ghost, and the drama in unfolding reveals the course of action he is to follow in interpreting the Ghost's lead. A creature from another realm has informed him of facts he could never have learned in the normal way of things and has enjoined him to a certain course. Young as he is, he is accustomed to do his own thinking, and while the course he will follow will not differ from one he would have set himself had he discovered the crime through natural means, the intrusion of the Ghost compels him to sound all he has ever been told of Heaven and Hell, all he has been told about his, or anyone's, presence in the universe. What might have been a fearful enough responsibility is weighted now with the need to search into metaphysics and theology. A being from another realm has brought with it proof that the concerns of that other realm may not be excluded from the conduct of affairs of the Court of Denmark. The Ghost has pressed upon Hamlet and his friends and upon the audience the sense of a strange other world that will not let this world be. Hamlet himself is perfectly well disposed to entertain mysteries, to acknowledge other than human powers, and to credit Heaven and Hell and diabolic and angelic beings. Moreover, he is plainly accustomed to honor traditional teaching and ecclesiastic injunction even as he pursues his endless questionings. He is at once a believer and confident of his own lucidity. Subject to stress after stress, to the very end he credits divinity and reasoning equally. And yet the inevitable, terrible conclusion is that neither faith nor reason satisfies his questioning or points him the way to righteousness. He comes to rest in reflecting upon his ignorance of the purposes of the powers that have him at their mercy.

For him as for the audience these powers reveal the ambiguity characteristic of divinity particularly when justice is attributed to it, and in demanding an execution the Ghost exaggerates the confusion. A mortal is being asked to perform an act appalling enough when demanded by Deity, as when Jehovah requires the sacrifice of Isaac, and the horror is increased when the request is made in order to satisfy a person, even if that be the spirit of a man's father. Whether the Ghost be from Purgatory or Hell, and whether the slaying be sacred or accursed, we fear with Hamlet the killing would accomplish nothing. Hamlet might think Jehovah is making a covenant with him, but for this he needs an assurance he never gets.[2] Lacking that he is left to himself, to what he can think through for himself and what circumstance makes possible. As the play ends we see Shakespeare following along with Hamlet, allowing the matter to be settled in a general turmoil.

And if at the end Hamlet should persuade us in the beauty of his spirit that it is not Fate but Providence that has been at work in the mists out of which he and all others have come, governed in their least motions by a benevolent agency, this only emphasizes to the point of intolerable irony his powerlessness. In the confounding of all purpose and all planning, in which even Hamlet's killing of the King is little more than a passionate retort, the sense of it all is lost. If this is the way Providence designed it, the results are no less confusing to the understanding of Hamlet, and of the audience, than the purpose the Ghost announced at the beginning. One cannot know if it is a good or an evil God that will be served, he becomes God's agent in being gulled.

Hamlet is, in short, forced back upon himself. Father murdered, mother unfaithful, beloved traitorous, the immediate villain impregnably placed, there is nowhere to turn, he has been cut off from kind, and even the friend he can speak to as freely as to himself cannot bridge this chasm. 'I am alone.' The Ghost does hardly more than emphasize his loss of the support of the closest ties of blood and love. So he must think for himself, think to the end, if necessary to the very edge of nothingness.

To be forced back upon himself—by shock and revulsion, by the unconsidered dishonoring of a too-trusting daughter, and by obligations as potentially corrupting as they are fruitless—this isolation immobilizes him. The only assurance, left to himself, that could have brought him to kill the king was the assurance of divine approval, and Hamlet's reasoning does not lead him to conclude that a good God would require that of him, even the son of the murdered man. He does not find in the Ghost's words the assurance that revenge would propitiate the spirit of the dead father and please God. He knows a troubled spirit has demanded propitiation, and inferentially he acknowledges the claim pity makes upon him for the sufferings that do not allow the spirit to rest. But even such piety as he feels for his Hyperion-father, and his disposition to bring criminals to justice, do not persuade him to drench himself in blood—as the conspirators in Rome exult in doing—in the hope of washing away his or anyone's guilt. He can act quite easily as a casual striker-down, in hot and in cold blood, of fools who annoy him, as callously as a man inured to killing in battle. He is as content with the code of duelling as a fire-brand, Laertes or Fortinbras. But murder as sacrifice, as a votive offering, as propitiation and cleansing, this is not for the man who resists defiling himself. The stage does not provide him with an altar.

More than once Shakespeare's figures have been caught in the worst of dilemmas—Antipholus, Cassio, Hermione—the lack of a witness to testify to probity, but only one, Romeo, was in a position to unpack his heart with deeds. Not even Prospero is more intoxicated with the love of God than Hamlet, but Hamlet is without help. He knows it, and in the end he makes peace with his knowledge. He uses the conventional words that signify not so much resignation as a willingness to comply with God's use of him, willing to accept the possibility that God's scheme cannot be comprehended, and that it is enough to trust to the course of time.

So when Horatio bids him farewell, imagining some heavenly rest for him, he confirms us in what we think we understand of Hamlet's faithfulness to his idea of eternal justice and of what that justice would demand of humans and of how it would make its demands. His tragedy accordingly is that of a man in a world where evil as it were casually disarranges the lives of many, where the love of good persists passionately, and remains immaculate, and where the world by its very nature makes it impossible for the good man to effect only goodness. Hamlet may be uncertain of life after death, or of its character, but he never doubts God's rule and never will consent to disobey. It is the clarity of his understanding that leads him to accept the state that is the properly human state when it is unassisted, having no truck with delusion.

Hamlet comes to terms with his thought in all that its clarity reveals to him. And the play proceeds in representing that process wholly sympathetically, with no distance between the playwright and the play. All that happens is as it would be seen by Hamlet himself if he had known all the circumstances. The tale is told as Hamlet would tell it, the play put on as in fact Hamlet puts on his. Told by another or contrived—by Ophelia or Gertrude or Horatio, by such as Gower or Old Time or the actor speaking the epilogue for Prospero or for Shakespeare—all could have been a tragedy in which the exaltation of spirit that follows upon the contemplation of the despair and the destruction of the good and the noble, would make for a tragedy with what we think of as the classic effect. But here there is no purification because there has been no defilement, and the serenity at the end is not that of the spirit transcending despair but of the spirit still appealing to thought.

II

In the crowded worlds his plays present we frequently think Shakespeare is making something of a force and power at work that in life we should think of as fortune or as fate. Unlooked for occurrences forward or ruin the best laid plans and we imagine imps at work. Sometimes a more certainly definable power seems to hold all in iron control. In tragedies and comedies both, many an utterance and circumstance points now to fortune, now to fate as the ultimate disposer, although many times when the indications are the clearest neither the persons in the play nor we are certain which it is. Pericles found armor cast up by the sea at the very moment it was needed to advance him towards the perfection that was his destiny. Antipholus found his twin and father and mother one by one in a distant city, and somehow so many lucky chances seem more than that. As the plays delight us with these suggestions of fate and providence and the sense of wonder we are led to reflect upon the possibility of still other agencies, whether there are beings called gods, or their ministers, directing fate or fortune, or else as much their subjects as the humans appear to be. Kent can swear by Apollo, Macbeth dreams of cherubim, Venus appears off Paphos, and sometimes it seems that as in Homer they too are among the armies of unalterable law. Or then again, they may be stirring the pother themselves.

We know well that in pointing to the certain importance of any such ideas we can badly oversimplify the character of the plays. The idea of fate properly brings with it the idea of law in effect everywhere, in the lives of men and in the world. Fortune may often signify something less embracing, mere randomness or coincidence, but it can also stand for a truly patternless succession of events. There are times, of course, when a play brings forward a sense of the authority of one or the other of these principles that we would not ever gainsay. We know that in *Macbeth*, for example, we must treat with the idea of fate as responsibly as it is possible to where so much points to the validity of prophecies, and where in the deterioration of character we see the inevitable consequences of sin. But we are as conscious of the possibility of irony in these suggestions as we are of doctrine, and even in such impressive words as Macbeth's

> Life's but a poor player that struts and frets
> His brief hour upon the stage

we perceive that he is imagining a role for himself even while we feel the terror in the words that say that humans are powerless to play any other parts than are assigned to them. So Caesar's

> death, a necessary end,
> Will come when it will come,

tells us of the temper of this great man so profoundly conscious of the public that is hanging on his every word even while the words suggest what could be the burden of the play itself, that even the gods are powerless before the indignities done their favorite. Each of Shakespeare's plays is of course held and formed by governing conceptions, but never, I think, are we able to say that these are so simple and clear that we can identify them as fatalism or as a particular doctrine of Providence. Even the ascriptions of religiousness can only rarely point to dogma.

Yet in the nature of things the plays are orderly, and in the representation of events the order always depends upon at least one idea we take to be unexceptionable, that our thoughts about what we are observing, as life itself and the events of the play, proceed in necessary ways. The plays may allow us to defer indefinitely any interest that arises in the question whether fate or fortune is ordering the characters and happenings that are holding our attention but we are never being allowed to doubt that what is happening does so because it has to. Should that assurance fail, the play fails, and we turn our attention to something else.

In *A Comedy of Errors* and *A Midsummer Night's Dream* we see persons taken with the sense that they are being carried along as people feel they are in dreams, and it may very well be that *Hamlet* communicates most strongly of all the sense of humans taken up by an indefinable yet inescapable power to their certain doom. So in the questionings of Antipholus and Lysander and Ferdinand, thinking they are living in a dream, they keep supposing some all-governing, all-pervading influence which they may refer to as fate as often as not, but I do not think the plays themselves can be taken to demonstrate that fate is all-powerful, or that it is the form God's will takes. However trapped this or that person in the plays feels, our attention and delight depend on the deferral of any such conclusions, our wonder deriving not from certainty but in the ignorance of what remains to be known.

We see a power at work in the passing of time and in the sequences of events which compels things to be as they are. What happens happens because it must, we identify this power as necessity. We become certain of its present workings, and we can often predict what it will occasion. We remain forever ignorant of the original impulse, although we may suppose there was one, and

even particular causes of known effects often elude our understanding. Differently than when we credit the way things are to
fate or fortune, any schematizing we are drawn to remains rudi-
mentary, and the principle will not permit itself to be assimilated
into philosophy. The indeterminate we are obliged to recognize as
an inherent component. Bradley put it rightly:

'Two statements . . . may at once be made regarding the tragic
fact as Shakespeare represents it: one, that it is and remains to us
something piteous, tearful and mysterious; the other, that the
representation of it does not leave us crushed or rebellious or
desperate. These statements will be accepted, I believe, by any
reader who is in touch with Shakespeare's mind and can observe
his own. Indeed such a reader is rather likely to complain that they
are painfully obvious. But if they are true as well as obvious,
something follows from them in regard to our present question.

'From the first it follows that the ultimate power in the tragic
world is not adequately described as a law or order which we can
see to be just and benevolent,—as, in that sense, a "moral order":
for in that case the spectacle of suffering and waste could not seem
to us so fearful and mysterious as it does. And from the second it
follows that this ultimate power is not adequately described as a
fate, whether malicious and cruel, or blind and indifferent to
human happiness and goodness: for in that case the spectacle
would leave us desperate or rebellious. Yet one or other of these
two ideas will be found to govern most accounts of Shakespeare's
tragic view or world. These accounts isolate and exaggerate single
aspects, either the aspect of action or that of suffering; either the
close and unbroken connection of character, will, deed and
catastrophe, which, taken alone, shows the individual simply as
sinning against, or failing to conform to, the moral order and
drawing his just doom on his own head; or else that pressure of
outward forces, that sway of accident, and those blind and
agonised struggles, which, taken alone, show him as the mere
victim of some power which cares neither for his sins nor for his
pain. Such views contradict one another, and no third view can
unite them; but the several aspects from whose isolation and

exaggeration they spring are both present in the fact, and a view which would be true to the fact and to the whole of our imaginative experience must in some way combine these aspects.'[3]

The idea of the necessary, in drama clearly, appears in the form of sequences that suggest the working of cause and effect as we know that in experience. Whether the work represents the likely or the preposterous, it always treats with the necessary. In the most fanciful stories our attention is excited by the expectation of consequences which in their occurrence we recognize as conforming to such conditions as mechanical operations themselves set. But this is not simply an intellectual interest, our expectations in anticipation and in suspense look towards satisfactions in delight. The more deeply engaged our feelings, the deeper we appear to understand the relationship between the laws of force and the powerlessness of humans. And so the playwright in imitating, meaning to interest and satisfy and delight us, leads our expectations on with hints of what is possible and probable. He is continually changing the direction of our expectancies, and he raises doubts. He continually holds out the possibility that the subjects of his imitating are free from some constraints, and in his resolution he may even lead us to wonder whether freedom and constraint are not the same, as Bruno has it.[4] Which is to say that the proceedings of drama as drama impose upon us the sense of the power at work in the proceedings of necessity. The sequences of drama, manifestly contrived, are able to suggest the sequences of experience itself because they appear to illustrate the processes through which causes obtain effects. All happens as it seems it would have to.

> As flies to wanton boys are we to the gods,
> They kill us for their sport.

In Plato's *Laws* a speaker simply designated the Athenian is led to ask, 'May we not conceive each of us living beings to be a puppet of the Gods, either their plaything only, or created with a purpose—which of the two we cannot certainly know.' (644 D).

He goes on to refer to so much in our lives that point to influences over which we have no control. In time the figure he drew upon became one of the commonplaces of human thought, taking various forms, in which humans are spoken of as actors in a play performed upon the stage of the world, or figures in a dream or a procession, coming into being and passing away according to some scheme devised or, if not devised, manipulated, by mysterious forces. And while as a commonplace it has enriched thought and imagination immensely, the figure may be as important in revealing the nature of rationality itself, the power humans have of looking upon themselves as it were from the outside whereby thought appears to take on the attributes of sight. In Longinus, among the ancients, we see how in speaking of one activity the language almost immediately adduces the other: 'Nature judged man to be no lowly or ignoble creature when she brought us into this life and into the whole universe as into a great celebration, to be spectators of her whole performance and most ambitious actors. She implanted at once into our souls an invincible love for all that is great and more divine than ourselves. That is why the whole universe gives insufficient scope to man's power of contemplation and reflection, but his thoughts often pass beyond the boundaries of the surrounding world.' (*On the Sublime*, translated by Grube, 35).

Whether the origin of humans is credited to the gods or Nature, or to powers less definitely named, any figure that points to them as toys or actors implies a master or an author. It thus implies distinct orders of existence, the one peculiar to humans and others apart from that. The figure invites us to examine the carefulness and fullness of our reasoning even as it develops the authority of the idea that has called for the comparison. It develops the image of someone looking at us from the outside, an all-discerning observer, one who may be our creator. Further, the idea and the metaphor, in identifying the two realms, propose explanations of the relations between the two, and, oddly, they imply the existence of still another realm. For, as Longinus remarked, in what inheres to it in the likeness to sight thought enters vistas beyond those in which we imagine the gods, taking a position from which it can even look upon them as it were from afar. Timaeus seems not to think it foolish to declare that 'such was the mind and thought of God in the creation of time' (38), as if he were privy to God's mind and detached from it. He may not care to make much of the literal sense of his words, but in the mere playing with the idea he has indicated the breadth he requires of thought.

Reason thus naturally arrogates to itself such power and authority, and there does indeed seem to be no limit to its province once it has embarked upon the notions this figure inspires. But religion is equally dependent upon the same conceit, particularly as men are moved to assign their origin to forces other than their own. And again, the question the Athenian raised presses itself as insistently—How free are humans? How free are they from the constraints of the powers that called them into being? Are we merely the playthings of the gods, or have they granted us some purpose to which we may contribute, that at least they will not prevent us from fulfilling?

Reflection, we know, does take place, and whether we shall ever succeed in knowing what Plato's Athenian says we cannot— whether there is a purpose to our being—nothing shakes our conviction of the activity of influences upon our lives. However pervasive these are it does appear that we conceive of ourselves in the act of thinking to be at a point of rest, so to speak, moving neither in space or time, which is as much as to say, independent of any influence from within or without. We use the words disinterested and detached to define this supposed state, whether it is truly what we take it to be or not. But whatever the truth of the matter, we treasure the thought of being free just as this image allows us to, and it may be that the figure of life as a play does at least demonstrate that thought in conceiving of necessity discovers its own freedom.[5]

But even as we explore the ideas and meanings the figure in Plato and Plotinus and the dramatists of the Renaissance develop —of 'this insubstantial pageant'—absorbed in discovering the richest discriminations in the schemes of things in which we can imagine that humans play a part, we may become so absorbed that we lose ourselves in the imagining. We know that for there to be knowledge there must be a union of the knower and the known, and paradoxically the figure that commences with the assumption that we may look upon ourselves as from a place apart ends by enthralling us—so it is with Prospero, dazzled by his vision, 'Sir, I am vexed, bear with my weakness.'

A similar irony controls the playwright's conception of drama where he would have his audience as critical in assessing the proceeding of the work he presents to us as he is himself, and at the same time he is undertaking to interest us so thoroughly that at times at least we shall all but forget ourselves. So man, in Longinus' reasoning, brought by Nature into the universe to apprehend its farthest reaches, in the process becomes ecstatic.

With the figure of speech as with drama itself we are always advancing and retreating, at one time scrutinizing our very reflection, at another absorbed, yet in the continuance of our attention in this fluctuating state there is a certain constant element, a certain wonder. All we are ever persuaded to take for knowledge, for truth, all delight, returns us to the Athenian's 'we cannot certainly know'; having advanced as far as we do in our discoveries we are held quite as fixedly with the majesty of what we do not know. In the delight of every newly established understanding, in the realized expectancy, we retain the sense of something still to know, our wonder ready to comprehend even the refutation of what we have just taken to our hearts. Enthralled, we yet know that we are still ourselves. We are—again with the Athenian—attracted by a sense of purpose. Our awe itself assures us of our own dignity even though we are conscious that our union with what we are intent upon is not complete. When we are most ourselves it seems that we still remain outside ourselves. In the great commonplaces of human wisdom, in philosophy and poetry, in the myriad of assurances that make up our lives, in all that excites our wonder we find ourselves returning again and again to the original concern, the discovery of the extent of our freedom, and this is why, when we study the satisfaction we take in tragedies, we ponder upon the nature of the hero's defeat. Could he have triumphed? Could he have escaped? Was it fated to be this way? The same question takes another form in any beautiful composition—is it this way and precisely this way through some divine necessity, as Leonardo spoke of it, or in the lovely surprise of the exactly right word and tone and color and movement is there something beyond what will ever be reducible to law? And so when we go on from philosophy as such to reflect upon these matters in the composition of works of art and the questions of fatality and freedom there that concern us when we reflect upon the nature of reason, we know we are meeting with the same question.[6]

Drama as such need not project or be a projection of a conceit—just as the children's dance of Ring-around-a-rosie for them need never be other than motion and song and ritual. But immediately there come into the drama words that refer to other kinds of existence, and particularly that of the gods, we shall not be allowed to forget that the drama itself depends upon the conceit and is illustrating it.

Obviously any writer knows he is leading us to compare the semblance of a thing to the thing itself, and by his art he may wish to lead us to confuse illusion and reality, even to discovering such pleasure in noticing the semblance that for a while we are persuaded that the world of his imagining is the very world of all of us. All artists have our uncertainties as ally in enticing us to lose ourselves in their imitations and inventions, to exploit our confusion about what is real and what is not, and in particular our fears that when all is said and done we may be no more free than puppets. The story of the Three Bears enthrals us with the reflection that the little girl need not have taken any one of the steps that brought her into so rigidly regulated a world where the bowls of porridge and the chairs and the beds were scaled precisely to the size of the bears. The conditions of that world are as fixed as those of a nightmare and yet the little girl's freedom is certain.

The pleasure we take in this as in all art is at once in the representation of the apparently necessary ways of things and with the unexpected and the surprising, and all this turns back to that initial question once again—is the representation of inter-linking causes a sure or an uncertain sign of the fatality of things, are the creatures in the fiction like us, the created and manipulated figures of a sport, or are they revelatory of a purpose and an end to their existence?

When Gloucester speaks of humans as playthings of the gods he is thinking not only of men as powerless and insignificant but of the gods as conscienceless and without any meaningful plan, killing their playthings at will. Their power is in this realm at least absolute, like fate's, and there is no hint that there is any meaning to their existence, that their lives accord with intelligible principles. Nor is there any indication of the opposite. So in this variation of the image of life as a play put on by supernal powers just as much as in Prospero's assertion that life is a pageant that dissolves into nothingness, the beginning and reason of it all remain a mystery.

The philosophers and prophets and theologians will speak somewhat differently. Plato will conceive of a Demi-urge bringing into being and directing the universe in the light of divine principles. Longinus will speak of Nature putting on the play and directing it to the glory of God. The Stoics and Neo-Platonists and Paul and Aquinas and Calvin will unfold systems of thought in giving authority to the image of the great stage of the world upon which an infinity of dramas are being played out. But they also will come up against the unknown ultimately, some origin in the backward of time, and they will be as duly respectful as the persons of Shakespeare's plays are of what resists codification. A great while ago—the song that ends *Twelfth Night* says—the world began, and things have happened as they had to. This we can know, the rest we must leave to wonder, but philosophers and some others will sometimes offer ultimate explanations.[7]

The ancient idea of necessity evidently took origin from the sense of the effect of force. Then, in Homer and Hesiod and the philosophers, as conceptions were developed of the character of matter in its response to force, the idea of necessity was extended to explain the results of actions upon the life of humans and of society and history. In the course of time the explanations become comprehensive and subtle. In the Renaissance the word and the conception were interwoven in the speculation about fate and destiny and fortune, in the developments of astrology and magic as well as in the reasonings of theology. And the issues, so vital to drama—obvious enough, for example, in *Julius Caesar* and *Romeo and Juliet*—treat here with as many of the discriminations as do the philosophers and theologians.

The concept of necessity had been profoundly explored by others before Plato, most impressively, it is said, by Parmenides, but for subsequent thought certain ideas of Plato were most obviously influential. Probably his most dramatic representation was in the Myth of Er:

'. . . in the midst of the light, they saw the ends of the chains of heaven, let down from above: for this light is the belt of heaven, and holds together the circle of the Universe, like the under-girders of a trireme. From these ends is extended the spindle of Necessity, on which all the revolutions turn. The shaft and hook of this spindle are made of steel and also partly of other materials. . . . The spindle turns on the knees of Necessity; and on the upper surface of each circle is a siren, who goes round with them, hymning a single tone or note. The eight together form one harmony; and round about, at equal intervals, there is another band, three in number, each sitting upon her throne: these are the Fates, daughters of Necessity, who are clothed in white robes and have chaplets upon their heads, Lachesis and Clotho and Atropos, who accompany with their voices the harmony of the sirens—Lachesis singing of the past, Clotho from time to time assisting with a touch of her right hand the revolution of the outer circle of the whorl or spindle, and Atropos with her left hand touching and guiding the inner ones, and Lachesis laying hold of either in turn, first with one hand and then with the other.' (*Republic* 616–7).

The conception of creation in the *Timaeus* is as important, where it is said that 'everything that becomes or is created must of necessity be created by some cause'. (28a). And after we are offered the stunning 'Such was the mind and thought of God in the creation of time' we are given a particular account: '... the creation is mixed, being made up of necessity and mind. Mind, the ruling power, persuaded necessity to bring the greater part of created things to perfection, and thus and after this manner in the beginning, when the influence of reason got the better of necessity, the universe was created.' (48a).[8]

We are here being apprised of much that has to do with the nature of matter, of the power of form, of purpose, of vastly complex reasoning, but even in the briefest summary we discern the driving conception, that there is a power informing that which responds only to power. 'These are the elements, thus of necessity then subsisting, which the creator of the fairest and best of created things associated with himself, when he made the self-sufficing and the most perfect God, using the necessary causes as his ministers in the accomplishment of his most perfect work, but himself contriving the good in all his creations. Wherefore we may distinguish two sorts of causes, the one divine and the other necessary, and may seek for the divine in all things, as far as our nature admits, with a view to the blessed life; but the necessary kind only for the sake of the divine, considering that without them and when isolated from them, these higher things for which we look cannot be apprehended or received or in any way shared by us.' (68–9a).

The sense of the Athenian's metaphor of the puppets is that men may despair or they may live in good hope, and they shall never know which is called for. The uncertainty in which they exist demands of them that they endure whatever comes, either with resignation or in the thought that 'all things that come from the gods work together for the best for those who are dear to the gods, apart from the inevitable evil caused by sin in a former life.' (*Republic*, 613a). Necessity may or may not define destiny.

This is to say that anyone who uses this figure in order to deepen his understanding and to compose himself must do so with the utmost seriousness, and in the recognition that, forced to make a choice, he may make the wrong one and by thus mistaking matters will be inviting madness to help in his destruction. He is also recognizing that the powers who oversee his life are remote, and they may be so little concerned that he may be completely on his own. On the whole Gloucester does not overload the burden of the figure as we are given it in the *Laws* for the form in which the Athenian puts it allows for the condition of humans to include the torture of either uncertainty or madness. Gloucester's apparent assurance gives only the momentary comfort of supposing he can do without hope.

Longinus, Plotinus, and many others may direct the figure into hopeful meanings and will be able to give cogent grounds for their conclusions. The Epicureans and the Stoics, on the other hand, may use it to underwrite their pessimism. Taken up by Christians of various kinds it may be similarly limited, where the persons in the play may believe some are destined for felicity, some for damnation. For some the divine powers will be infinitely remote, for others they become fellows. But whatever the variations in all their significances, the figure serves the central purpose of bringing forward a conception of reality in helping to make known the terms on which humans can and must live with it. Not only with Plato, but with all, the figure depends upon the conviction of pure Being, the grounds of all determinations, of all existence, that which abides when the play is over with and the actors disposed of.

And so we discover that what is a figure aiding thought is also an index to the nature of rationality, bringing with it the postulates that support the doctrine that the knowledge of the order of things is accessible to reason. Hamlet may be less certain than Gloucester that the gods have no interest in the plays they are observing if not instigating but as much as Gloucester and Prospero and the philosophers he is enthralled by the conviction of powers at work and of Being beyond the shoal of time.

The figures in the play are ignorant of the means of their begetting, of the burden of the play, and of their function in it. But they have come to think they are in a play and this leads them to ask not only who begot them and why but what they can do to escape committing themsleves to illusion. They are impelled to entertain the thought of reality, to endeavor to participate in it, to suppose they may become one with it. They are urged to this in part from an innate disposition to search out truth (it is this that has informed them of illusion), and in part because life as they know it contains such misery and is evidently doomed and they with it. In short, they are urged on by the thirst for felicity and immortality.

Most philosophers insist that the actors in the play have been given parts, and it is up to them to learn how to play their parts. Performing properly—perhaps I should say perfectly—they will succeed in participating ultimately in the divine being that has occasioned their existence. This will come about only as they devote themselves to their perfection and only when in the course of nature the play has come to an end.

There is also present the belief that that which gave them their existence does indeed watch over them and either wishes their perfection or is careless of it. But whatever else is to be said of this power it is not knowable, not immediately accessible, its purposes are not to be fathomed. Accordingly, the actors in the play can have no other guide than the play itself as they come to know it by performing in it. They learn their parts, the persons they are, they learn of the action in which they are all joining, and they perceive that what is taking place is to be understood as of necessity, that it could not be otherwise. Such freedom as they have is in obedience to what they discover this to be. Finding it useless to seek out that which occasioned the play, they are left to discover its conclusion for themselves. The figure of the play therefore is an expression of loneness, abandonment, madness, despair, and urgency.

III

Gloucester's sense is that as playthings of the gods all men are powerless before forces that torture and destroy us arbitrarily. The horror is precisely in what is said in Plato, necessity is blind.

Contemplating the intolerable, Kent cries, 'Is this the promised end?' Edgar supposes even worse—'Or image of that horror?' Lear in the terrible irony imagines Cordelia and himself as God's spies, ticking off the goings and comings of the fools who think life is theirs to make of what they will. Edmund vaunts his sufficiency—'as if we were villains on necessity, fools by heavenly compulsion'—but the turn of the wheel shows him as deluded as any. The gods may drag the play out or they may tire of it quickly but they know only one ending.

Lear is unusual in that the references are almost exclusively to the gods' direct manipulations. There is almost nothing said of the intermediaries that we see and are told of in other plays. Here unaccommodated man comes to terms with his fortune neither helped nor hindered nor warned by witches or ghosts or fairies or avenging angels. These apparently tangible presences, both in the comedies and tragedies, make it possible for other persons to entertain the thought that the ultimate powers are treating with them in specific and intelligible ways. The witches in *Macbeth*, the ghosts in *Julius Caesar*, Ariel in *The Tempest* bring with them clear notions of fate and destiny and justice. In act and word they suggest a defined principle at work in circumstance—Reason acting upon Necessity. They may even suggest that the world is providentially governed. The witches accentuate the possibility that law is being executed in Macbeth's destruction; the spirit in *Julius Caesar* suggests that an implacable justice is punishing the murderers of the most god-like of men; and when Ariel identifies himself as a minister of destiny we are asked to believe that God is exacting specific penance of the sinners. Yet in the end these untoward beings—ghosts, apparitions, whatever their nature—are at least as enigmatic as the gods Gloucester was imagining. We are never certain what it is they authenticate.

There are a few rare occasions, especially in the last plays, when an apparition speaks unmistakably for the ultimate power. In the vision in *Cymbeline* when Jupiter says 'Whom best I love I cross', the authority we acknowledge in those words makes of them more than the expression of a merely fanciful being, and

points to the God of Christians. This *deus ex machina* has answered
the enigma with an assertion whose meaning one may not qualify.
Generally, however, the intermediaries only serve to defer the
mystery, leaving us with the original question, variously and most
richly bodied forth, even exulted in playfully, but never answered
—is necessity wholly blind?

As a significant aspect of so many of the dramas the idea that
life is a play or a pageant is not restricted to notions such as
Gloucester's or Prospero's, that humans are pulled and hauled
about and obliterated in spite of themselves, for quite as provok-
ing are the suggestions of powers working within humans,
working within their nature and character, as the finally con-
trolling impulsions. Macbeth's picture of himself as a poor player
bears the sense of a force shaping his consciousness, impelling the
sounds he utters, even dictating the images that come into his
mind.[9] This sense of the power within, proceeding according to
its own laws, challenging or defeating every conceivable effort at
autonomy, is most conspicuously delineated in the reasoning of
lovers. Proteus, Helena, Hamlet, Miranda—the list is long—will
often enough suggest that love between man and woman, or
parent and child, or man and God, is the fullest expression of
inclinations and desires and aspirations, and there is even the fear
it may be despotic.

Berowne had spoken prophetically at the beginning of *Love's
Labour's Lost*—'Necessity will make us all forsworn.' (I. i. 147).
His reasons were sound enough:

> For every man with his affects is born,
> Not by might mastered, but by special grace.

(149–50)

'Mastered by grace' would mean 'miraculously' and yet of course,
by the very power of love to temper passion, not harshly but
according to the sweetness of its nature and the worth of what it
serves. At another place we meet with the idea that this is no
miracle, this is the way of Nature:

> . . . Nature is made better by no mean

But Nature makes that mean. So, over that art
Which you say adds to Nature, is an art
That Nature makes. (*The Winter's Tale*, IV. iv. 89–92)

But even when we think Shakespeare would have us reconcile the differences, conceiving of grace as the perfection of nature, I think for him it always comes down to this, that love, to be true to itself, submits itself to what brings harmony to the universe, 'the fated sky'.

.... love, first learned in a lady's eyes,
Lives not alone immured in the brain,
But with the motion of all elements
Courses as swift as thought in every power,
And gives to every power a double power
Above their functions and their offices.
(*Love's Labour's Lost*, IV. iii. 323–8)

Again and again Shakespeare shows that the distinction between 'the affects' and love is that between compulsion and what is freely chosen. When Pericles, who has promised the most holy love to the daughter of Antiochus learns of her evil, in an instant he can say, 'Good sooth, I care not for you,' (I. i. 86), and is freed to turn elsewhere. Love evidently depends upon the will, and the will agrees with love only when it knows its object to be good. This is as it is in Platonism generally, and in scholasticism as well. In Shakespeare, even with Antony and Cleopatra, we see lovers challenging and influencing their passions. Not even Othello is so much the slave as any of the heroes and heroines of Racine and Tasso, where the passions are identical with Omnipotence—for them the mere thought of freedom is a mockery. In Shakespeare love may always alter in the passions what would otherwise be blind; serving the good and beautiful, it works in harmony with what is free in humans and what is noble. Helena expresses this doctrine as well as anyone in countering even the fates:

Our remedies oft in ourselves do lie,
Which we ascribe to heaven. The fated sky

Gives us free scope; only doth backward pull
Our slow designs when we ourselves are dull.
What power is it which mounts my love so high?
That makes me see, and cannot feed mine eye?
The mightiest space in fortune nature brings
To join like likes and kiss like native things.
Impossible be strange attempts to those
That weigh their pains in sense, and do suppose
What hath been cannot be. Who ever strove
To show her merit that did miss her love?
(*All's Well*, I. i. 206–17)

Ficino spoke of an *ars intrinsecus* in nature,[10] and Shakespeare shows that he too thinks of the counsels of love as counsels to be trusted. Florizel in *The Winter's Tale* asserts the bond between love and truth, freedom and goodness, in as defiant a challenge to fate as Helena's—

Or I'll be thine, my fair,
Or not my father's; for I cannot be
Mine own, nor anything to any, if
I be not thine. To this I am most constant,
Though destiny say no. (IV. iv. 42–6)

All such defiance is an appeal to a still superior power, some excellent authority life itself is believed to honor. These lovers believe, as was said of Pericles, they are among those on whom perfection waits. Many are proven wrong, and it is chaos, not perfection that awaits them, yet even in the confusions of Troilus and Othello one may judge that it is not love that has failed them but their regard for truth. The tragedies quite as much as the romances bear out the doctrine Berowne took from Scripture, that charity fulfils the law. It is when men betray themselves that the passions and necessity proceed to exact their cruel price. They are true to themselves in being true to what informs human love with an intuition or a knowledge of perfection. In sum, 'charity fulfils the law' signifies that the heart has reasons that Reason does not know,[11] not that love is above the law.

This is a lesson lover after lover learns in these plays from the earliest time on, but it is so deep a learning that the fullest explanations are developed slowly. Not only philosophies of nature are involved, for the sanctions of religion will also be called on as the various characters come to speak of the power swaying them. Shakespeare in the beginning may have learned from the Neo-Platonists and from Bruno, but his Christian upbringing would have given him as much. Berowne is being witty and casuistical in speaking of love as charity, however fine a sense he has of the excellence of the love of women. But neither *Love's Labour's Lost* nor any of the plays in themselves trifle with the idea. It is sounded if not the most profoundly the most abstractly in *The Phœnix and Turtle*. The tragedy of Denmark is in its dishonoring.

Men reason as well as they can, making such sense as they can in the gallimaufry, but consciousness itself, as the King says, is a continuing and uncertain effort, and the squaring of the world with sense and reason even through love is a desperate venture:

> There lives within the very flame of love
> A kind of wick or snuff that will abate it,
> And nothing is at a like goodness still,
> For goodness, growing to a plurisy,
> Dies in his own too-much. That we would do
> We should do when we would; for this 'would' changes,
> And hath abatements and delays as many
> As there are tongues, are hands, are accidents,
> And then this 'should' is like a spendthrift sigh
> That hurts by easing. (IV. vii. 114–23)

What Claudius has said alludes to a general principle. If good itself is vulnerable to excess, then no circumstances could provide what Hamlet needs to purify Denmark, himself, Ophelia, Gertrude. If what Claudius said applies even to love, the defection of all is in the nature of things—in the motions of elements, in their functions and their offices. But Hamlet can never refer everything to nature so regarded—to take up the thought of

Claudius, goodness and love and truth perishing like flame in its own surfeit. All that Hamlet sees takes form and lives and dies not in the way of nature but of another order of being in which the extremes are salvation and damnation. What to others is seen by the light of nature he sees by another light—

> And is't not to be damn'd
> To let this canker of our nature come
> In further evil? (V. ii. 68–70)

At other moments it is angels and ministers of grace crowding about him. In the terrible words, 'Leave her to Heaven', the Ghost counts on Hamlet's seeing his own reviling as so much more than that, and so it becomes:

> Heav'n hath pleas'd it so,
> To punish me with this, and this with me,
> That I must be their scourge and minister.
> (III. iv. 173–5)

Every thought is rich with the light shining on 'the undiscovered country'.

All his judgments are enveloped by the sense of 'the outer world',[12] but it does not tell him everything he wants to know. In *The Tempest* Prospero will conceive a number of images illustrating the life of divinity that all but express the sense of time and space obliterated. But Hamlet never, I think, crosses the threshold into those realms that the words 'dark backward and abysm of time' and 'baseless fabric of this vision' refer to as reality. Yet the sense of them must have been beating in his mind.

In the reunion with Rosencrantz and Guildenstern the thought of old times was refreshing to Hamlet, it brought back remembrances of the sweetness of life outside his prison. The players reminded him of more still, and when he thought of what they had once meant to him and of that life now over with, it occurred to him that past and present, the forgotten and the actual, might be proceeding in such a way as the plays he once knew. Suddenly his mind took fire, and for the audience, at the same moment, the drama takes fire. Until this moment it is as if Hamlet's mind were idling. First there was a moment's stillness, but when the players left he exploded. The currents piling up broke the dikes, and there was the terrible outburst—

O what a rogue!

Until now all had been preparation, infinitely rich, of course, in thoughts and pictures—the magnificent quiet at the changing of the guard; the dark; the Ghost; the mention of a cock crowing on Christmas Eve. Then the scene with the king in full splendor, blotting out the mention of drunkenness and squalor. Until now this marvellous 'tight dispersion' has been an index to we hardly knew what, and now the play runs on with its own momentum, and Hamlet's staging of the Mousetrap, his plot to twist the screws, all merged into a spectacular succession of incidents in which he himself appeared to be as helplessly driven as the creatures he played with in his thoughts—John-a-dreams, the cursing whore, the peasant slave.[13] And at the same time he was playing the part of the producer of the play, assigning the parts and overseeing the actions.

Until now Shakespeare's work had passed before us like an introductory scene in which the author let us know he was setting the stage, and now the dramatist himself is caught up in the conception of the power moving his protagonist about. The dumb-show, merging into the play that followed it, is primarily responsible for this effect.

Mr. Dieter Mehl observed that before *Hamlet* it is only in *A Midsummer Night's Dream* that a dumb-show precedes a play-within-a-play, in that instance accompanied by comment that announces the nature of the action that is thereafter to be represented more fully.[14] A speaker by the name of Prologue allows no misunderstanding:

> Gentles, perchance you wonder at this show;
> But wonder on, till truth make all things plain.
>
> (V. i. 126–7)

In *Hamlet*, of course, the antecedent show intensifies the suspense that forms as its deviser makes certain it will—'this is miching malhecho; it means mischief.' (III. ii. 131). And when this Prologue enters Hamlet says it again, 'The players cannot keep counsel; they'll tell all.' (133-4). In *A Midsummer Night's Dream* the Prologue was concerned to allay suspense, to allow no fear to trouble the courtly audience; here the intent is to commence and justify fear. In both plays the effects are complicated through action performed as it were on a multiple stage, the play-within-the-play being offered alongside the audience for which it is being performed. But in both productions there is the same fundamental conceit, an event recorded in the past is being offered as taking place in the present—myth and history become pantomime, pantomime becomes tragedy, and the courts of Athens and Denmark are caught up into the very representations put before them. Members of the audience sitting and standing on the stage find themselves acting out parts in the play they are watching. But also the audience in the theater, we ourselves, seeing Claudius startle, seeing the play of Gonzago broken off, seeing Hamlet moving towards some other course, find ourselves looking upon ourselves as having become part of still another play. First we were one with Claudius and the Queen watching the audience, and at the same time one with Hamlet and Horatio watching them. Then, when some of these ceased to be audience and were swept up into a play that was neither Hamlet's nor the Players' but Shakespeare's, losing the parts that had been given us we could only think of ourselves as carried along by the circumstances Hamlet now encounters.

This shifting of our roles and perspectives confounds any distinctions we had been able to keep between the creatures of imagination and those of actuality, but when so very much is presented to us as play-acting, as pretense, we find ourselves coping with an abstract question, what is the relation between the imagined and the real? A play supplied with words following the dumb show—itself as parody an almost diabolical conceit—has represented conceit as taking on the form of actuality.

Shakespeare's, Hamlet's, the Ghost's, Necessity's instigations and plots, devices all, are so mingled that for each and all it could be said,

> [their] whole function [was] suiting
> With forms to [their] conceit. (II. ii. 540–1)

So, it has been said, Claudius has been 'dragged as if by a nightmare into the drama presented for [his] entertainment.'[15] But the result goes deeper: 'Claudius sees at the same moment an image of his crime and a foreshadowing of his own death. In effect, this simultaneity is a promise to the audience (the larger audience, not that of the courtiers in the play)'—I should say, to them as well—'that justice will be done,' 'death [being] inherent in sin and the punishment in crime.'[16] The audience has seen conceit followed by form, pantomime by the remembrance of murder, the imitation of murder by fear, and seeing fear drive Claudius from the stage we have been brought face to face with the knowledge that judgment attends all. The fiction has been turned inside out. Usurping function conceit became truth.

> Only we die in earnest, that's no jest.

This progression from pantomine to play to fact brought Claudius and us to look at the face of death and at the truth in horror.

Throughout the drama we were asked to think about the world and human life as if it were a thing apart, as if the planet and all it contains could be looked at as a whole—in the wonderful phrase, beneath the glimpses of the moon. The Ghost and any number of the references to Heaven and Hell are part of all that kept before us the notion of a number of worlds and of a wealth of perspectives. For us this came to signify above all else the idea of the transience of human life, the sense of its coming into being and passing away.

It appears that from antiquity on the thought of life as a play and of the world as a stage brought with it the sense of a point of observation neither in time or space. The language is paradoxical, of course, but the attraction of the notion of glimpses from the moon or the depths of Hell is probably in that disposition to detach ourselves from concern that we call ironic. The idea of life as a play is such an irony, only in the nature of things a falsification humans cannot afford. In Raleigh's word, this is no jest. This was the most serious point Plato's Athenian was making.

Proposed provisionally the conceit offers a saving power to our hopes, even ironically again, as with Gloucester, proposing we may do without hope. Developed, it may move us with the pathos through which we continue to love the earth we know to be too-much loved. But its supreme value is in the promise it makes to help us distinguish between dreams and truth, between sleep and waking. Professor Jacquot concluded that the ancients and the Church Fathers developed substantially all the meanings that became attached to the figure and that the humanists of the Renaissance added little of substance.[17] Perhaps the most fruitful development of all had been in Plotinus:

'. . . the Soul, entering this drama of the Universe, making itself a part of the Play, bringing to its acting its personal excellence or defect, set in a definite place at the entry and accepting from the author its entire role—superimposed upon its own character and conduct—just so, it receives in the end its punishment and reward.

'But these actors, souls, hold a peculiar dignity: they act in a vaster place than any stage: the Author has made them masters of all this world; they have a wide choice of place; they themselves determine the honour or discredit in which they are agents since their place and part are in keeping with their quality: they therefore fit into the Reason-Principle of the Universe, each adjusted, most legitimately, to the appropriate environment, as every string of the lyre is set in the precisely right position, determined by the Principle directing musical utterance. All is just and good in the Universe in which every actor is set in his own quite appropriate place, though it be to utter in the Darkness and in Tartarus the dreadful sounds whose utterance there is well.' (III. 2. 17).

Plotinus was calling to attention the underlying conception that as much as anything, I believe, made the conceit intriguing, the sense of the stratum of Being, the ultimate substance that we must refer to when we conceive of coming into being and perfection as the activity of the universe itself. It is the sense of this that Hamlet points to in conceiving of the bank and shoal of time. But he falls far short of the assurance of Plotinus, far short from believing that as a creature of the wide world's dreaming he is at one with all that's just and good. He also lacks, and Shakespeare's play lacks, the assurance of Ficino, identifying Plotinus's Providence with the Christian. God, Ficino wrote, has called our souls into life, some to take part in a comedy, some in a tragedy. But whatever it is to be, it is all unreal, a fable—riches, poverty, kingship, slavery, birth and death, these are all unreal. The life of humans upon earth is a play of God's (*Dei ludus*). He, who is the father of our souls, is the author of the play. From above he provides the actors, and the nature of the world itself gives them their parts.

Ficino goes on to tell his friend he should not grieve for the death of his son, for he was not his creation, he was God's, it was God who gave him his part to play, and it was only a part in a play, not life itself. It is now that he is truly alive, returned to true life (*uitae substantiam*), and having played his part in the play honestly and reverently his true father is giving him an eternal reward.[18]

The idea does not signify this in Shakespeare. The creature that appeared to Hamlet comes not from the depths of Tartarus, a fiction, but from reality itself. Evil here is not to be conjured away as the Neo-Platonists could think, for whom salvation was an assured reward. The end of *A Midsummer Night's Dream* makes the point Shakespeare will always make—evil is always ready to intrude.

When the Ghost appeared, we were compelled to think of the realm it came from and to which it returns, not exclusively as Hell or Purgatory but as that state in which through mysterious impulsion the soul of one who has died is given form, and a message with which to haunt the living. There are of course all the suggestions of theology but there is also the question of the subsistent reality, in fact of precisely such a state as Plato's Athenian and all the classic philosophers conceived of that was not illusion. Marston took the trouble to define what he took this to be as 'the boundlesse *Ens*'. In *Hamlet* Shakespeare lets us think this might be such a

metaphysicis as orthodox theology, or for that matter unorthodox
—as with Calvin—could affirm.

In discussing the great importance of the play metaphor for
Renaissance thought and drama Miss Anne Righter made a most
important distinction. She contrasted the idea so important to
Renaissance dramatists, that dramas, in Hamlet's phrase, hold a
mirror up to nature, with her sense of the character of the medieval
mystery plays. These, she said, were 'a glass held up towards the
Absolute, reflecting the "age and body of the time" only inci-
dentally.' '. . . the fourteenth-century playgoer was urged to
associate illusion with his own life and Reality itself with the
dramas enacted before him.' In these plays it was as 'within the
walls of a mediaeval church, as within the mind of God Himself,
"all time is eternally present".'[19]

She concluded that as time went on Shakespeare came to be
revolted with the play metaphor, as a device and in its substance,
and that *The Tempest* reveals his revulsion. 'Now, the barriers
have been swept away altogether; the play metaphor, like the
distinction upon which it was based, no longer exists. As Prospero's
explanation reaches its end, the audience in the theatre seems to
lose its identity. Life has been engulfed by illusion.'[20] For me it is
the other way round. The conceit continued to look towards truth.

NOTES

[1] W. M. Merchant, 'Shakespeare's Theology', *A Review of English Literature*, V (October, 1964), 82.

[2] I believe one should give considerable thought to the view of Mr. Harold
Fisch although, as I see it, he presses the point too far: 'The great stage
play which is ultimately intuited by Hamlet and for which the grave-
diggers provide us with the essential terms is no other than the covenant
history of the world, considered as a great plan of Providence unfolding
in a Biblical dimension of time and place.' (*Hamlet and the Word, The
Covenant Pattern in Shakespeare*, New York, 1971, p. 165).

[3] *Shakespearean Tragedy*, London, 1922, pp. 25–6.

[4] 'The necessity and liberty of God are one and the same and there is no need to fear that when He acts according to the necessity of nature He is not acting freely; He would not be acting freely were He to act otherwise than necessity and nature, or rather than the nature of necessity requires.' (*De Immenso*, I, xii; *Opera Latine Conscripta*, ed. Francesco Fiorentino, Naples, 1879, I, 243). '. . . le Premier Principe promouvant hors de soi l'univers où il s'exprime, toujours presént (en tant que nature, comme la Diane des *Fureurs héroïques*) et toujours dérobé (en tant qu'universel Apollon), fait jaillir le possible du nécessaire mais, au delà du nécessaire, demeure inconnaissable en sa souveraine liberté.' (Paul-Henri Michel, *La cosmologie de Giordano Bruno*, Paris, 1962, p. 91).

[5] I believe Aristotle bears this out when he says of the love of wisdom: 'We do not seek it for the sake of any other advantage; but as the man is free, we say, who exists for his own sake and not for another's, so we pursue this as the only free science, for it alone exists for its own sake.' (*Metaphysics*, 982b).

[6] Mr. J. V. Cunningham cites an interesting passage from Albertus Magnus that carries on the Aristotelian concept of the end of poetry as wonder in terms that point to the commonness of purpose in the arts and philosophy: 'Thus Aristotle shows in that branch of logic which is called poetic that the poet fashions his story for the purpose of exciting wonder, and that the further effect of wonder is to excite inquiry. Such is the origin of philosophy, as Plato shows with respect to the stories of Phaeton and Deucalion. The single purpose of these stories is to excite one to wonder at the causes of the two deluges of fire and of water (which issued from the circuit of wandering stars), so that through wonder the cause would be looked for, and the truth discovered.

'Hence poetry offers a method of Philosophizing. . . .

'. . . we define the man who wonders as one who is in suspense as to the cause, the knowledge of which would make him know instead of wonder.' (*Woe or Wonder, The Emotional Effect of Shakespearean Tragedy*, Denver, 1951, p. 80. Citing the *Commentary on the Metaphysics of Aristotle*, in *Opera Omnia*, ed. Augustus Borgnet, Paris, 1890, VI, 30a–1a).

[7] One of the most concise reviews of the history of the idea of the world as a stage in philosophic writing is that of Jean Jacquot, '"Le Théâtre du Monde" de Shakespeare à Calderon', *Revue de Littérature Comparée*, XXXI (1957), 341–72. I should only like to add here a note of Professor Roy Battenhouse: 'Calvin views God and His angels as the spectators while men play rôles assigned and directed by the author of the pageant.'

('The Doctrine of Man in Calvin and in Renaissance Platonism', *Journal of the History of Ideas*, IX (1948), p. 464).

8 'It is in the *Timaeus* that Plato makes his most determined effort to represent the origin of cosmic good and evil. Here the dualism is complete. God, the Demiurge, Providence, *Nous*, soul, represent the living, intelligent, purposeful source and agencies of good; and the resistance to the divine act of creation comes from the blind, inert, recalcitrance of "necessity" or matter.... Wishing to find a teleological explanation of *physis*, and noting that such powers as *Ananke* and *Heimarmene* have hitherto been generally conceived as hostile to man, he has resorted to *Nous* as the reason of things being well disposed. So Plato, too, opposes God's will and goodness to the works of nature, *Nous* to *Ananke*.... "Now what we have said thus far, save for a few things, has displayed the creations of Reason (*Nous*); but our discourse must also set by their side the effects of Necessity (*Ananke*). For the generation of this world came about from a combination of Necessity with Reason, but Reason overruled Necessity by persuading her to conduct most of the effects to the best issue; thus, then, was this universe compacted in the beginning by the victory of reasonable persuasion over necessity."' (*Timaeus* 47e–48a). (W. C. Greene, *Fate, Good, and Evil in Greek Thought*, Cambridge, 1944, pp. 303–4).

9 I illustrate this matter in *The Art of Shakespeare*, London, 1964, pp. 41–50.

10 *Theologiae Platonicae*, IV, i, in *Opera* [1576], p. 122).

11 Mr. J. W. Lever described finely the remarkable comprehensiveness of Shakespeare's thought in the claims he made for love in the Sonnets: 'The operative faith in these sonnets has been centred upon a love growing out of sense-perception and personal experience, subject to "all frailties that besiege all kinds of blood", yet transcending the world of sense through the power of the human spirit.' (*The Elizabethan Love Sonnet*, London, 1956, pp. 271–2).

Mr. A. D. Nuttall in a sustained argument has corrected the common suggestion that Shakespeare's references to the infinite value of love are merely hyperbolical. Here I can only mention one of his conclusions, for the argument is wide-ranging and deep. 'For Shakespeare, love is not so much a way of blotting out one's cares as a way to transcend them. He celebrated not a lowered but a heightened consciousness. His horror at the flux of things is like the horror which Plato inherited from Heraclitus and Cratylus, in that it is universal, and only to be comforted by eternity. If we follow the plain sense of Shakespeare's words, a metaphysical interpretation seems inevitable.' (*Two Concepts of Allegory*, London, 1967, p. 124).

I also believe the argument of M. D. H. Parker, though supported by less exact analysis, is persuasive in referring Shakespeare's conception of reality to an orthodox Christian eschatology. (*The Slave of Life*, London, 1964, pp. 176–7 in particular).

[12] Professor R. H. West has written most rewardingly on this—*Shakespeare and the Outer Mystery*, Lexington, Kentucky, 1968.

[13] Mr. R. J. Nelson writes: 'It has been through illusion (the apparition sequence) and pretense (the play within a play) that Hamlet has explored reality, through them that he moves toward the definitive act by which he will revenge his father's murder and restore well-being to rotten Denmark. The real which has given itself as pretense (the "antic disposition" and "The Murder of Gonzago") has undone the pretense (Claudius' hollow reign and his feigned concern for Hamlet) which has given itself as real. This fundamental irony of *Hamlet* is preserved in the final playlike structure of the play, Claudius' own mousetrap, the fake dueling match of Act V. Once again Hamlet does something while appearing to do nothing: he turns the fake into the fatal. But has he not always proceeded in this manner? The "play" or "show" of action has always had a real purpose for him. "Hamlet is so much of a professional," writes Mark Van Doren, "that the man in him is indistinguishable from the mime. His life as we have it is so naturally and completely a play that we can almost think of him as his own author, his own director, and his own protagonist."' (*Play within a Play*, New Haven, 1958, pp. 27–8. The citation is from Van Doren's *Shakespeare*, New York, 1939, p. 281).

[14] *The Elizabethan Dumb Show*, London, 1964, p. 110.

[15] Anne Righter, *Shakespeare and the Idea of the Play*, New York, 1969, p. 163.

[16] Cicely Havely, 'The Play-Scene in "Hamlet"', *Essays in Criticism*, XXIII (1973), 225, 228.

[17] 'Le Théâtre du Monde' de Shakespeare à Calderon', *Revue de Littérature Comparée*, XXXI (1957), 359.

[18] *Epistolarum Liber VIII*, in *Opera* (1576), I, 884.

[19] *Shakespeare and the Idea of the Play*, pp. 14 and 15.

[20] *Ibid.*, p. 203.

Dream, Vision, Prayer:
The Tempest

From the first, watching the spectacular storm and the crazed behavior of those aboard the ship, we are not moved as we might expect to be by drama in which the representation is so vivid. There is a great 'noise' that should be drowning every voice, yet as the sailors and passengers curse and pray and even jest their words come through as it were unweakened, and there is as much of the ridiculous as the desperate in what we hear. Then, when the storm subsides and we join the two who have watched it from the shore, going over with them all that has been happening, we learn how little there was indeed to fear. The cracks of sulfurous roar, Jove's lightnings, Neptune's boldness were no more harmful than the St. Elmo's fire that was not even that but the guise Ariel had taken to bring it all about. And in the words that tell the real enough distress of those who thought God was punishing them we come to recognize the act of a power moved as much by concern as anger.

Brought into the quiet where Prospero and Miranda are watching, we are hardly surprised to hear music, whether from the air or earth, leading a young prince out of the sea to before the feet of these two.

> Come unto these yellow sands,
>> And then take hands.
> Curtsied when you have and kissed,
>> The wild waves whist,
> Foot it featly here and there;

And, sweet sprites, the burden bear.

(I. ii. 375–80)

We have learned of powers effecting wonders at sea, at the same time lightening fear and gracing the terrible, and now there are signs of what might be still others, loving and gentle and humorous. A young fellow rescued from the very heart of a tempest finds his spirits suddenly rapt with beauty.

Where should this music be? I' th' air or th' earth?
It sounds no more; and sure it waits upon
Some god o' th' island. Sitting on a bank,
Weeping again the King my father's wrack,
This music crept by me upon the waters,
Allaying both their fury and my passion
With its sweet air. (I. ii. 387–93)

It is not Ferdinand's bemusement that suggests divinity at work in this disembodied music so much as the words with which Ariel embodies it. In their simplest sense they are wonderful enough—bearing an invitation and promising an unthought of satisfaction, blessing a betrothal more kindly than even the magnificent songs ending *Love's Labour's Lost*. But the words are also prophetic, and it is in this character that they are the strangest for they speak as if present and past and future were in a single moment, leading Ferdinand on step by step while telling of something that is yet to happen as by one who has already seen it come to pass. The words seem to belong outside time.

To add to what Prospero tells us about Ariel we are being led to think of him as someone like a sorcerer's medium who knows more than anyone possibly could unless consciousness inhabited the very nature of things and took a voice. But the most provocative indications that Ariel has commerce with another, mysterious realm of being are in the song he next addressed to Ferdinand:

Full fathom five thy father lies,
Of his bones are coral made,
Those are pearls that were his eyes,
Nothing of him that doth fade

> But doth suffer a sea change
> Into something rich and strange.
>> Sea-nymphs hourly ring his knell.
>> (I. ii. 396–402)

This is mockery—Ferdinand's father is alive, still walking the earth. No one rings his knell, least of all the nymphs that never were. And Ariel himself, 'beginning it', ringing the bells, is enjoying this playful way of leading Ferdinand on, persuading him he is surviving and is his father's heir, and that in a little while he will be making Miranda his queen, death leading to this joy too. Ariel is taking delight in the idea, in the fancy and fun, in the deceit, and in the happiness he foresees for the young prince. He is also celebrating a most wonderful power and act, imagining transfigurations in which a body and a skeleton by the grace of the all-sustaining sea have become jewels and marvellous sea-growths. Besides the mockery and the fun, besides the fancifulness and the factuality—that in the course of nature death distributes its mortal objects among the other forms of the world—there is the astonishing clarity of his perception. In the mere naming of eyes and pearls and bones and coral he endows them with such beauty and strangeness as we would not have known the objects of sense possess. It is this clarity Milton responded to so directly in picturing the jewel-paved streams of Paradise, water and stone becoming turkis-blue and emerald-green and azure, the lucidity all things own when honored rightly. All is seen by such a light as Ariel says will be his forever after he has left Prospero's service—

> Where the bee sucks, there suck I,
> In a cowslip's bell I lie,
> There I couch when owls do cry,
> On the bat's back I do fly
> After summer merrily.
> Merrily, merrily shall I live now,
> Under the blossom that hangs on the bough.
>> (V. i. 88–94)

As Prospero prepares to give over his last responsibilities, thinking of his grave, he imagines a time when all else will have disappeared in a rounding sleep. His sense of things now is the opposite to the burden of Ariel's song that death is the means of transformation into the rich and strange, and in that 'nothing' he speaks of in the dead, that nothing that will fade, we also read, endless, ceaseless change. It is Prospero who is speaking at the end, and we may think the play is concluding in pressing his assertion of the vanity of all things even though his words are not unambiguous.

But the irony in his conclusion is sharp enough, as it also is in the epilogue, to keep us from forgetting the continuing existence Ariel was planning, an almost impish defiance of any constraining power whatever—

> Merrily, merrily shall I live now,
> Under the blossom that hangs on the bow.

Earth's increase, revels, marriages and christenings may all be done with, now and forever, when the globe is gone, but from the time of that first sight of Ariel's work and his first singing we are kept mindful of an illimitable spirit, a capacity whose limits are unknown. His strange knowledge, the resonance of his words, his power not only over the forms of matter but in penetrating minds, all seem to say he could do what he would—we cannot perceive what limits there would be for him beyond that vague contract with Prospero. And when Prospero with his gloriously beautiful words allows us to think there might be an end to all that humans have ever known he but re-invokes our wonder at what we have come to think is unconstrained. Ariel is no more to be bound, as unconstrained now as that power that transfigured a dead man, quick with what freedom makes possible, a power never to be a party to obliteration.

It is not only with the flowers of summer, or when freed from a curse, no longer subject to the pinchings of a master or the harassment of Caliban and the imps of the earth that Ariel, a delicate spirit, will joy in his liberty. He is assured he will be everywhere always, partaking of existence in every form nature and time and understanding take.

Prospero has used Ariel to perform miracles, to introduce dreams and madness into men's fancies, to chastise, to condemn, to guide, and Ariel has of himself conceived and devised what he needed in managing these most difficult matters. And like the songs he ornaments his work with, all he does pays as full respect to the way things are as it does to the playing of the imagination. He will be as free and immaculate as light and will thereby honor thought and being as much as nature.

As the drama moves towards its end, and the Milanese and Neapolitans prepare to return to the mainland, Caliban is being left behind to whatever his lonely future, and Ariel has disappeared. But nothing leads us to think he is vanishing into any such darkness as Prospero prophesies for humans. He has simply been let go, to exist as he knows existence—wherever it is, however to be thought of, it is inseparable from light.

A magician avenged himself and arranged a decent future for his daughter. Approaching the end of his life he began to prepare for it. He looked back upon it all as the evanescent thing it was, as all earthly life, full of illusion, passing traceless from all knowledge.

His own labors had been finally successful, partly fortuitously, partly through real spiritual insight and the power that had been lent to him, provisionally as it were. He had pursued justice, and executed it upon the wicked and the shameless, he was returning Milan and Naples to order and the promise of a decent future. The usual uncertainties were to be anticipated but meanwhile he had been just and merciful. And even though in the course of his precarious and difficult undertaking he had brought forward the most sustained and searching reasonings to support his faith in a God of justice and mercy, he knew well enough he had accomplished no more than any proper magistrate would have. And so it is that I think we are to take his valedictory as one might take anyone's—an affirmation that he has done as well as he could, it was not good enough, he has not effected what divinity itself would have, and with his own passing all may foresee their own.

But his language remains pretentious, it is full of the metaphysical affirmations he and much of his enterprise had depended on. So we must accept his declaration as much as ever as by his lights, and not identify it as the burden of the play—he is a bilked old man who succeeded in settling a claim and thinks he has earned a rest.

He may of course have been as capable of divine intimations as anyone, as his author, and his author may not too ironically for a moment or two allow himself to be brought forward in Prospero's words as someone whose life was also writ on water. But there is also the author who more obviously introduces himself in the Epilogue as someone not identical with Prospero, offering a belief to take the place of Prospero's philosophy. This figure suggests that the end of life may be another life. Prospero may have believed, until he was disabused, that for faithful and perfect service salvation was to be his reward. But the words of the epilogue say something else—the soul devoted to thought, to the service of philosophy and justice, is still imprisoned, and the freedom that is eternal life thought itself cannot earn. Prospero has done well, the dream of efficacious power was rightly enchanting, but it was a dream, the idea that he could do God's work. The suggestion has been denied that virtue would take him beyond the sphery chime. If he is to wake it will be through God's free act.

> But how is it
> That this lives in thy mind? What seest thou else
> In the dark backward and abysm of time? (I. ii. 48–50)
>   We are such stuff
> As dreams are made on, and our little life
> Is rounded with a sleep. (IV. i. 156–8)

The words 'dark backward and abysm of time' and 'rounded with a sleep' invite speculation upon realms of being 'outside' that the senses and even thought know. The very word 'outside' is paradoxical, since it signifies normally what is accessible to experience. Yet the language and matter of the play themselves compel us not only to treat with paradox but to accept what the paradox is founded on, the notion of a realm of unchanging being, the only basis that can be suggested as contrast to the world of change and time, a realm of the changeless and timeless. 'Certainly through Prospero's speech on the vanishing of the globe Shakespeare is not affirming that we last forever, but rather the exact reverse. Yet the nature of the denial is metaphysical in its assumption of pathos. It only makes sense in the context of immortal longings.'[1] Leaving aside whether it is Shakespeare or Prospero who is thought to be affirming this, the question persists—in this conception, in these dim figurings of 'abysm' and 'darkness' and 'roundness' is there a power the poetry and the play sustain deriving from an assured metaphysics?

The subject and the question were with Shakespeare from the beginning. They took a charming form in the humor of the Princess of France when she repelled the too importunate pleas of the suitors, deferring an answer, this being

<blockquote>
A time ... too short
To make a world-without-end bargain in.
(Love's Labour's Lost, V. ii. 774-5)
</blockquote>

In the Sonnets, as Mr. J. W. Lever so well rehearsed it, human love has truly deific power:
'... the co-existence of beauty and corruption, of truth and mutability, and the universal tyranny of Time, which were the issue of Shakespearean drama, became in the sonnets the issue of personal integrity; and through the prepotency of human love, on a plane customarily reserved for divine grace, a poetic resolution was affirmed for the antinomies of life.'[2]

Something very close to the wonder in the conception underlying these images in *The Tempest* is at the heart of the magnificence of *Antony and Cleopatra*:

<blockquote>
O sun,
Burn the great sphere thou mov'st in, darkling stand
The varying shore o' th' world! (IV. xv. 9-11).
</blockquote>

'The darkening shore, the determining centre of the world

dissolved, the obliteration of all that gives distinction and difference, so that the moon must look in vain for anything to invest
with mystery, abundance surfacing from the containing medium—
all this poetry has for its basic idea, not a particular bounding line,
but in widest conceivable terms the border between the formed
and the formless, that alien region with which a great part of the
poetry of the last plays occupies itself.'[3]

In Sonnet LX we read what we may take to be almost an out-
line of the conclusion Prospero has been led to:

> Nativity once in the main of light,
> Crawls to maturity, wherewith being crowned,
> Crooked eclipses gainst his glory fight,
> And Time that gave, doth now his gift confound.

The question arises—in such words as these, are we being
presented with metaphysics proposed responsibly, or are these
merely playful figurings, useful simply for teasing thought? And
then, since we meet with the same suggestions again and again in
the poems and plays, in an almost infinite sounding, even sometimes developed into arguments, is there some constancy in the
repetitions that would indicate a fixed disposition and cast of mind
if not belief of the author's? Or are these ideas that go to the heart
of Platonic and Christian philosophy being allowed to dissolve in
ambiguity? Professor Nuttall thinks that in *The Tempest* scepticism
took on a new life: 'It is as if a second wave of scepticism has
passed over the poet. It is quite different from the coprologous
indignation of *Troilus and Cressida*. He no longer, for the sake of
one transgression, denies the authenticity of love itself. But a
reservation as to the truth-value of the assertions love provokes
seems to have reappeared. Time, the old grey destroyer of the
Sonnets, was not, after all, put down by love. After the enthusiastic
reaffirmation of the later Sonnets and the first three Romances, a
sadder and more complex reaction has set in, slightly ironical
perhaps, but not at all cynical. The world has not been wholly
redeemed by love; look at it. The subjective vision of the lover
may transcend objective facts, but it does not obliterate them. The

lover has one level, the hater another; perhaps there are a thousand more such levels, each as unreal as the rest.'4

It is clear that throughout *The Tempest* we meet with many indications that the ultimate triumph of good is far from certain, for no more than in the tragedies is there any scanting of the power of evil and of death. Yet I do not think the ending effect is simply ironic or sceptical, or that the prayer of the epilogue is but the recognition of defeat in the face of the conclusion that all we love is doomed. Nor does Professor Nuttall think this is the conclusion we must certainly draw. The wonder suffusing the entire work is so powerful we must be sure we have made all the discriminations we can before unresolved doubt is accepted as the final suggestion the play is making.

For one thing, we must discover if anywhere in the play, or elsewhere in Shakespeare's writings, there are matters that not only bring us to a still closer comprehension of what we would judge to be not merely metaphysical speculations but religious commitments; if here and there arguments are so resolved that *il gran rifiuto* should seem inconceivable. Do the poetry and drama, through images and symbols, ever develop meanings that the arguments do not include? In short, are there conceptions evidently so religious that contradiction would leave them unaffected?

The 'dark backward and abysm of time' is paradoxically an image of space in which we are led to negate the idea of duration. The bottomless pit of the abyss, or else the formlessness of chaos, suggests endlessness in the other sense: our imagination, our memory, our sight, looking back to that dimly sensed time before thought came to life and light lost itself in the notion of endless space. And as the images of space and duration become confused we are compelled to try to conceive at once of nothingness and of the timeless, and of how there could be such a thing as coming-into-being—out of 'the jaws of darkness'.

'Rounded with a sleep' presents us also with opposites. The globe and all that inhabited it having vanished, life and consciousness are said to end. Yet that which we can only know as waking is said to be in sleep, and we are bound to infer, such sleep out of which waking has taken its life. Consciousness is ended as a circle ends, and that completion which is ending one thing is continuing that very thing; the annhilation of what we have taken to be life is yet the continuance of a sort of life. We vanish and yet sleep.

The reasoning underlying these paradoxes opposes on the one hand duration to timelessness and space to nothingness, and on the other, being to non-being. This reasoning is, I think charmed with the notion of perfect being (*ens perfectissimum*), the reality underlying all change.[5]

But it is not the abstractions of thought, or the appeal of metaphysics that are finally holding us through these words of Prospero's but rather the sense they establish of persons searching the abyss, or waking from sleep, images of particular persons taking the form of life. Miranda, of course, and Prospero, or ourselves, what it is that gives particularity to persons treating with each other and with reality. What holds us above all and will not let go is the sense that such words are saying as much as can be said of being born into the world of sight and touch and breath. We are drawn to wonder not at truths about Being but about the survival or disappearance of individuals, and, as some of the key devices of the play will make clear, about the nature of our own coming into being and passing away. The metaphysical substance is here but it is not without reference to the concern for individuals peculiar to religion.

Mr. D. G. James had this in mind when he wrote of what it was that Miranda remembered when her father appealed to her:

> 'Canst thou remember
> A time before we came unto this cell? . . .
> Of anything the image tell me that
> Hath kept with thy remembrance. (I. ii. 38–9, 43–4)

We see the mind fetching out of its past some fragment of our infant dream—"of anything the image tell me"—stumbling in the vast darkness of what lies behind us, in the immeasurable depths which lie beneath us; a sense of the incalculable immensity out of which our lives appear and with which they are continuous, which we know, but cannot contain, within ourselves. (We think of the second of those last chapters of St. Augustine's *Confessions* which M. Gilson has called the *Paradiso* of the *Confessions*, and the words: "Great is this force of memory . . . a large and boundless chamber. Who ever sounded the bottom thereof? Yet is this a power of mine, and belongs unto nature; nor do I myself comprehend all that I am.") Out of this vast darkness, Miranda brings the image of herself, royally attended.'[6]

Mr. James has taken the paradoxes—'immeasurable', 'incalculable', and yet to be known—and thinks it right to equate Prospero's notion of the abysm of consciousness and Miranda's summoning of her first remembrances with Augustine's *abyssum humanae conscientiae* (*Confessions*, X, 2), carrying forward what else the play has suggested of the Platonic metaphysics into Augustine's Neo-Platonizing and Christianity. I think we may agree that much in the play supports him in this although the dialogue itself may be thought to stop short. What gives his paraphrase the authority it does obtain is all that in the play is likening life to a dream. The subject is not only the relation of images coming out of the memory to the truth of things, or the likenesses of memory to the kind of thought that is called dreaming, it is also all that the play in telling of dreams and of truth, of illusions and reality, is treating with the authority by which an individual judges himself to be dreaming.

Prospero is to speak of life as a pageant, which signifies somewhat dimly but clearly enough a patterned procession of humans across time and space. The substance of the notion was his at the beginning when he was explaining to Miranda how those returning from the wedding in Tunis had come into his power. The moon, the tides, the plans of many persons, the coming of age of his daughter, all as it were conjoined.

> By accident most strange, bountiful Fortune
> . . . hath mine enemies
> Brought to this shore. (I. ii. 178–80)

What in his later perspective is a pageant is to those caught up in it a troubled sleep, a driven motion whose direction they cannot know. Prospero will also say that life in the pageant is an insubstantial stuff, that most if not all of the actors are dully sensitive, their reason muddy where it should be clear. (V. i. 82). Even 'things certain' (V. i. 125) they disbelieve. Yet knowing neither themselves nor what is driving them they are all too sure of suffering and confusion, of sorrow and loss, of hate, of crime, of being strangely manipulated.

> All torment, trouble, wonder, and amazement
> Inhabits here. (V. i. 104–5)

Prospero can look upon the pageant and the dream as if detached from it, although he concludes he is not, but the others never gain his wisdom. They are told of truth and the work of Providence, they did what they could to master confusion, but all they ever came to know was that they were powerless before mysterious impulsions, some learned they were being brought to judgment, and even to a beginning knowledge of themselves. (V. i. 212–213). All sensed the intrusion of mysterious forces.

As Ferdinand, Alonso, Gonzalo searched for clues to their predicaments we see in their uncertainty just such obscurity as faced Miranda. Confronting experience they cannot account for or comprehend, their memory itself confused, even what is before their eyes is 'rather like a dream than an assurance.' (I. ii. 45) Alonso, when told Prospero is his brother, hardly dares acknowledge what he might be expected to know if he knew anything:

> Whe'r thou be'st he or no,
> Or some enchanted trifle to abuse me,
> As late I have been, I not know. Thy pulse
> Beats as of flesh and blood; and, since I saw thee,
> Th'affliction of my mind amends, with which,
> I fear, a madness held me. This must crave
> (An if this be at all) a most strange story.
> (V. i. 111–17)

But it is of course Caliban's confusion as he recalls the celestial music that seemed to him the very rain of grace, when if ever it was truth, not a dream, that held him, causing him to pray to dream again. It is this that says most plainly of all how far everyone but Prospero is from what he will call understanding. Prospero's assurance, and, at the end, his serenity rest on his acceptance of the paradox, that we know change for what it is from knowing of changelessness. Miranda probably rests in wonder—which may be a deeper understanding still, and Ferdinand may learn to. The others must take on trust that what they do become assured of is for their good. They must believe it is right that they should become themselves again, but they will have no inkling of how it all began or ends, where it ends, or how the parts they played became theirs even though they themselves had chosen them like Plato's souls in choosing good or evil.

The strange necessities that brought these dim images into Miranda's remembrance were at work in what one after another took to be his dreaming. It was these same necessities in their apparent incoherence that Prospero solicited with his magic. We sense them in what we learn of the origins of Caliban, in the purposes of his terrible parent, in Ariel's history. There is an indication of the same strangeness in Prospero's likening the whole earthly existence to a pageant, a procession whose commencement is as undefined as its conclusion, though its existence and its passing are evidence of indeflectible compulsions. What all attempt to do is to take these strange stirrings to be life—their remembrances of the past that is the prologue, their existence which seems no existence, their annhilation which they do not succeed in imagining. So it is, I think, that we may not take Prospero's wonderful summing up of his conclusions as the play's, for what he says is but another dimly recognized shape taking form out of the abysses in his understanding, and the light by which we are to perceive this is not to take form until the epilogue. Other words of Augustine in the passage Mr. James pointed to apply as well to Prospero as to the others—'the mind is too narrow to contain itself entirely.' (X, 8).

In speaking of the end as a rounded sleep Prospero is in one sense using words to point to what may not be possible even to conceive of. In another sense he is applying to death a characterization one after another in the play was applying to his present life. Paradox, absurdity—whatever—the words signify limitation and constraint, the loss of consciousness, of the power to act, of freedom. Many in the play had been led to think their waking life not unlike this, and their acting as their inaction like somnolence. On occasion a charm transfixed them, but even without a charm there were occasions when they felt the helplessness men know in dreams. And in likening what they continued to think of as their waking state to this they felt they had lost possession of themselves, the dream no longer evanescent but, rather, all there was. However lightly sketched much in the play is, the import of this fear, and desire, was developed to the limit, to the conclusion Prospero drew. Powerlessness, confinement, the loss of consciousness. If there was illusion in all this it would have been chiefly in the thought that freedom had been wholly taken from the living. On the other hand, the fundamental irony of *The Tempest* is in precisely this, that it is not an illusion.

Sometimes one or another had an intimation of another existence entirely, apparently not transient but enduring, through hearing celestial music, or through a vision, or in the sight of what appeared to be gods. Sometimes circumstance, sometimes a succession of events seemed to testify to the reality of fortune and destiny and providence. But unless it was Ariel, no one was to rest for long in the assurance of anything other than bondage. Until at the end they were returned to themselves—as Gonzalo said, 'no man was his own.' (V. i. 213). Prospero alone entertained the thought of lasting non-existence—when his understanding had gone as far as it could he found a paradox to account for the time when he, too, would no longer be his own. Each thought of his confinement differently, and the conditions were indeed different, but on one matter all agreed, no challenge would disturb the rule of what was fated.

Long before the audience supposes anything like this to be

the burden of the play we are presented with a number of indications, apparently trivial in themselves, that are preparing for it. As the storm rages the boatswain curses the passengers who are getting in his way. Gonzalo reproves such insolence, offering the old joke that the rascal is clearly destined not to drown but to be hanged. Fate, if not society, he is suggesting, has ways of correcting license. There are other such instances of insubordination. We are reminded of the worst by Prospero's presence on the island, expelled from Milan by his brother. One reference after another establishes the very action of the play within a history of rebelliousness—Ariel had been locked into a pine tree because he would not comply with all that Sycorax required; Sycorax had been driven from Argier for outrages; her god, Setebos, would have been the most incorrigible of all—Caliban but inherited his and his dam's disposition. Never content they were all seeking to break free from the conditions life had set for them.

As such indications were multiplied we are bound to notice a certain consistency in the fortunes of the visitors to the island as they continue in the ways of insubordination and rebellion. Conspirators, having been successful in bringing down a duke, set out to kill a king. Confounded once, they set to again, they become desperate when they are thwarted this time, and imagine it is a legion of devils they must hereafter fight against. Seeking to free themselves from the limitations imposed by another's sovereignty they end in the prison of hysteria. Caliban and his new friends enjoy a wonderful exhiliration in their drunkenness, they think the island is to be theirs almost for the asking, and yet they end by being hounded as never before, and are returned to the same galling servitude.

There had been irony in Antonio's 'What's past is prologue', suggesting that the dispossession of Prospero was but an act in a drama leading to the removal of the King of Naples, a drama already written. He spells it out, this is destined—

> And, by that destiny, to perform an act
> Whereof what's past is prologue, what to come,

In yours and my discharge. (II. i. 245–7)

The nature of that destiny may not be what he supposes—Ariel saw it differently: destiny caused the sea to belch Antonio and his companions upon the island, caused them to go mad, even arranged for their perdition. Ambition in truth was everlastingly promising rewards for those who would overthrow authority in seeking more and more scope, and it appeared that it was in the nature of things for such attempts to lead but to other restraints. Such ambitions were misconceived, the world was inhospitable, and every success bore within itself the requirement of its own frustration.

What was true for the noble conspirators was also true for the others, each undertaking was self-defeating. Caliban's rebellions led to more scourging. Moreover, had he succeeded, Miranda ravished would have no more been won than Milan conquered was possessed. The ambitions of the good and the just were conceived in deeper respect for the ways of nature and destiny, but these too would fall short and discover their limits. Whatever promises love and the service of justice made, or seemed to make, the way of the world was still unfathomable, there was much no one could give direction to. Ferdinand and Miranda understood that in some sense they were discovering freedom in devotion, but for them, too, there was the long future with its mysteries that Juno and Ceres were to celebrate. Not only death but time itself would see to it that Prospero should put down his task. Ariel alone was assured of complete emancipation, but through means no human could even know of.

Who it is Prospero serves may not be named. It is certainly not a person, and not love, if that could be thought of as a power in nature or as a goddess. He can reasonably enough refer what happens to fortune and providence, even as if they were deities, yet we shall not find him using such words as those on the ship who pray when they see death coming near; or such as Ariel spoke in reminding the wicked of the need for contrition and satisfaction, words that point unmistakably to the traditional observances of

Christians and even to sacramental doctrine. He hardly ever allows himself such language as Ferdinand, that all the devils have left Hell in order to people the storm; nor is he ever to suppose, as the young prince does, that he has come into the presence of a deity. Prospero, of course, has summoned up spirits who take the form of Juno and Ceres—(Ariel represented Iris)—and in making it clear these are not the goddesses themselves he but continues his consistent reticence. He has proof enough of the reality of spirits, of the hierarchy of demons, of the terms on which spirit and matter treat with each other according to the complex of emanations in which all eventually derives from a single source. This everlasting, divine power he continually consults and obeys, and within the limits of his understanding he is able to conspire with it in effecting good. But whatever he himself brings about is only what force could have effected—transformations of mind and the growth of love he may encourage, but that is all, these proceed according to other necessities.

Prospero also knows how limited his understanding is. He may speak of the thoughts of others as 'muddy' (V. i. 82) and even promise their ultimate enlightenment, but he can only dimly apprehend his own future. His reason has in every respect informed him that there are abysses reason will never sound. No god—Eros or Chronos or any—will for him ever take form out of the abyss of being, no object will through the power of love inspire in him such promises as Ferdinand and Miranda treasure.

It was left to Ariel to delineate and celebrate all that Prospero holds in honor even if he himself is imprecise—the idea of a transcendent power that is also immanent, that shows the means of redemption and indeed authorizes them, that transforms the dead, that is assured of the existence of perfect freedom. But even Ariel does not give this power a name.

The idea that there might be something more to human exist-ence than conforming to the obligation of command and service, to law in whatever form, was first put forward in the loveliest of senses when Ferdinand knew himself enthralled to Miranda. Being goddess-like she drew his entire devotion, and so he took joy in the menial tasks Prospero set for him in order that he might not think he had gained this wonder too easily:

> There be some sports are painful, and their labour
> Delight in them sets off; some kinds of baseness
> Are nobly undergone, and most poor matters
> Point to rich ends. This my mean task
> Would be as heavy to me as odious, but
> The mistress which I serve quickens what's dead
> And makes my labors pleasures. (III. i. 1–7).

The piling of logs—'this wooden slavery' (III. i. 62)—thousands of them—becomes a patient nothing done in her service. It becomes a game, and more, a means of gaining heaven's favor—

> The very instant that I saw you, did
> My heart fly to your service; there resides,
> To make me slave to it. (64–6).

And Miranda, supposing the worst—that she will not become his bride—swears she will become his servant. (85). The two of them never tire of playing upon the idea of servitude—and so, finally, Ferdinand proposes marriage,

> with a heart as willing
> As bondage e'er of freedom. (88–9)

The language has made the meaning all but explicit—love transforms subjection into the enjoyment of power that ambition was always seeking—possession, union, exultation. Constraints cease to be known as constraints when content promises to follow upon content. All the insubordinate motions that looked towards power mistook their ends as they mistook their means. Instead of honoring what they would possess, they treated it with dishonor, seeking mere domination—reducing Miranda to an object, kingship to tyranny, loyalty to manipulation. Ambition, ever restless, never satisfied, was its own confinement. Even dedication to the work of justice could but set the stage for the correction of wrong since the unregenerate were free to remain so. Love, however,

endowed humans with the conviction of power extending limit-
lessly, even though much of what was to come would be unfore-
seen. In the ceremony blessing the betrothal of Ferdinand and
Miranda, Juno and Ceres tell them that such affection as theirs
nature itself blesses. Nature, bringing offspring, causing the earth
to flourish, forwards what divinity blesses, what love has indeed
prophesied. Those who love well are being told their faith is
sound whatever is to happen in the course of time.

This sense of being moved about despite themselves is in part
the recognition that particular efforts fail in their intent and have
disappointing consequences. In part, also, it follows from the
recognition that forces the characters are more or less ignorant of
are intruding in their affairs. Prospero himself acknowledges the
activity of powers he may be aware of only intermittently but that
he must believe are ever-present—the bountiful fortune that has
brought the ship to the island when he is able to make the most of
the opportunity to effect his purposes; the fortune, also, that takes
on the attributes of providence. There is the sense of an even
more instantly directing power in the consciousness of what time
brings about—the education of Miranda, the maturing of
Ferdinand, the period allotted for Ariel's service and the fixing of
the time for his emancipation. As impressive a witness of the
power of time as anything else is in our notice of the vision
Caliban has had of a celestial life, for in this we believe there to be
inherent the suggestion of a fulfilment possibly yet to come. There
is above all the ceremony of the goddesses, Juno and Ceres,
looking towards the fruition of nature through the years.

The sense of time passing and in its passing bringing to birth is
pressed upon us insistently, in innumerable circumstances, and
just as in Prospero's soliciting of Miranda's memories and the
sense his words there give of the womb of time, so the plotters
against his life express the same all-encompassing meaning—
'What's past is prologue' (II. i. 257). Even as it were in incidental
remarks the pervasiveness of the idea is made known to us, as
when Antonio speaks to his accomplice, suggesting the murder of
the sleeping king—

O, that you bore
The mind that I do! What a sleep were this
For your advancement! (II. i. 259–61)

In whatever circumstances, and with whatever emphasis or reference, this sense of powers and of powerlessness is but the extension into philosophy and superstition and religiousness of the theme struck in the first scene of subordination and insubordination, of the cost of responsibility, of the vexation of the ruled, of the desire for emancipation. Almost everyone is chafing at the bit—Prospero with his impatience, Alonso with his grief, Antonio and Sebastian like the boatswain and the drunken butler and Caliban himself in their self-willed ambitions. The desire for emancipation is conceived of not as freedom from the demands of power, but from the demands of authority. The slaves will become slave-owners, the lieutenants kings. Antonio's words fit them all— all except Ariel—

My brother's servants
Were then my fellows, now they are my men.
(II. i. 266–7)

Subject to the circumscriptions of existence, life and the dream as the images of fatality, in another dimension are images of the misery of the ruled—of servants and children and ministers, of all subordinates, of the dissatisfaction inherent in mortal life. As of Prospero himself before his expulsion—

Which first was mine own king. (I. ii. 342)

Even in humor Prospero returns to the theme, teasingly rebuking Miranda—

What, I say,
My foot my tutor? (I. ii. 468–9)

In the dream all are stupefied, in society all are goaded. Which is to say, for all that thoughts are free (III. ii. 118), for all—with spirits bound up—that minds may hold fast to visions or to truths or to justice or to enmity and hatred and rebelliousness, all in nature is confinement.

The world of master and subject, of nature and husbandman, the only world we do know, can be nothing else than one in which men accommodate themselves to each other and to the universe either in strife or in cooperation. It is folly to dream to escape to some state in which rulers are accountable to no one or any thing. The thirst for power can no more be freed from the constraints of power than the creatures of dreams may escape dreaming. The point is extended, and the question becomes from every viewpoint, is liberty an illusion?

The play begins in violence and with the threat of catastrophe, it ends in stillness, in happy and decent prospects, calm seas and auspicious gales. After the spectacular beginning there was an elaborate, even a drawn-out setting of the scene, renewing what the audience as well as Miranda need to know. We were then shown newcomers to the island devising conspiracies almost immediately, and we witness marvellous, even miraculous happenings. We were initially impressed with hints of what Prospero was planning to do, particularly as we learned of his extraordinary powers, but as the scenes succeed each other it is not this that focuses our interest so much as a series of encounters—Ferdinand meeting Miranda; the reuniting of the passengers from the foundered ship; Caliban's joining up with Stephano and Trinculo. We become interested in what these meetings are leading to, what enterprises are under way and how they may affect each other, and largely independently of our concern for Prospero's ultimate success.

Some of the encounters had been arranged, others had come about by chance. Sometimes they seem to have been the work neither of humans or spirits but of invisible influences that suggest the manipulations of fortune or destiny or providence. But in their succession there is so little to be thought of as a plot, the entanglements are so little constraining, that we see that in this play the imitation of the action is as Aristotle conceived of it—an imitation of the energy in life that moves towards fulfilments, or, when perverted, towards frustration. And so when Ferdinand comes upon Miranda, when Antonio and Sebastian and Alonso are reunited, when the clown and the drunken butler join up with the monster, we are but lightly held by such a knitting of interests that constitute a plot, and we are more held by what we see to be at work in the lives of those before us. By the growth of love in Ferdinand and Miranda ('It works'—I. ii. 493); by the energy and inventiveness of malice as well as by the limitations that show themselves to be inherent in evil (Prospero's foes hysterically pursuing legions of fiends); by the words of Ariel that for a moment we may take to be those of an avenging angel ('You are three men of sin.' III. iii. 53). Prospero, of course, has a plan he has plotted, and much comes about as he wishes, but there is so much more that is at work that we are prevented from identifying what he is devising as either the plot or the action of the drama. We are more held in discovering how love and the directions of nature conspire, how dreams may claim authority, how character as well as magic perform charms ('They are both in either's pow'rs'—I. ii. 450) and, above all, we are held by our developing sense of something not to be defined that may be giving direction to all this.

In the various meetings now one now another moves to advance his purpose. Prospero sets Ferdinand tasks that will teach him to value what he hopes to gain, Antonio and Sebastian grab at the chance to murder Alonso and Gonzalo. Successes and failures alike require other undertakings, and the actions in their various stages are as it were punctuated either by apparitions or an account of what might be at their root, as when Ariel sings fancifully of the death of Ferdinand's father, and when Caliban remembers a vision. The apparitions themselves—a banquet appearing and vanishing, evocations of harpies and hounds, goddesses performing a ritual—cap as it were this or that incident with a symbolic reference that attests to the moral and spiritual issues that have arisen in the course of the action. In their sum they attest to still something else, to the continuous presence of the powers ultimately responsible for the existence of what is appearing before us, being themselves translations of the events of the play into expressions of another order of existence. They illuminate the nature of the action of the play, what it is that is giving the lives of the characters their directions, what makes of it all, in Prospero's term, a pageant.

Prospero instigated several of the ghostly appearances and, knowing we may suppose, their import, but what is said by the figures in the apparitions would seem to have gone beyond what he could have conceived. Ariel, most especially, carrying out his orders, speaks as from someone within the vision, addressing sinners as if possessing divine authority, while Prospero can at most, and from the outside, approve. And what Juno and Ceres do in blessing is beyond what even a magician could hope to perform. Then, too, these marvellous sights, accompanied so often as they must have been by music from unseen instruments—as it was when Ariel with her singing led Ferdinand to Prospero and Miranda—would seem to have taken form in another world. By that very suggestion the import they bear would seem to possess something of the character of the chorus in ancient drama, not submerged in the circumstances of the drama's action but granted the special power that belongs to truth itself—comprehending, judicial, serene.

In addition to their spectacular nature many of these marvels hold us with the sense of the same mysterious and fascinating power of so many of the images of the play, the same strangeness that stirs us in Prospero's words asking Miranda to search her memory, and in what goes so far beyond the commonplace when he recalls the infant's smile that encouraged him when the two were adrift—

> O, a cherubin
> Thou wast that did preserve me! Thou didst smile,
> Infusèd with a fortitude from heaven,
> When I have decked the sea with drops full salt,
> Under my burden groaned; which raised in me
> An undergoing stomach, to bear up
> Against what should ensue. (I. ii. 152–8)

But nothing, probably, speaks more for the importance of this power in defining the interest that holds us in the unfolding of the action than Ariel's song to Ferdinand telling what has happened to the dead.

The words begin in tolling, 'Full fathom five,' and then out of the fearful beat there arises a strange beauty. We are struck with the preposterousness of so swift a change of bones and eyes to among the loveliest of sea-growths. But in the startling we recognize too the truth of what we have always known, that in death as in life there are continuous transformations, all is to be wondered at, all changes being preposterous, always to be expected and always surprising. And in these lines there is the promise of the most astonishing marvel of all, that the man himself will take another form, and not merely his bones and eyes. With such apparent guilelessness promised such beauty, such marvels, led into still more expectation, and especially of the strange, the words inevitably strike us with the suggestion of a mystery in what is being done, in the course of things, and in what it all is to end in. In what might have been simply a beautiful mocking song, some celebration of something like the jewel-paved streams of Paradise, we are held by the sense of power at work, transforming and transfiguring the remnants of a man and the man himself.

Nothing is more important to the marrying of the marvellous and the natural than what the production of the play would owe to spectacle and music. The storm scene with its great 'noise' is succeeded by the sight of a young prince rescued from the sea and led to safety by music that enraptures him. Music and singing interrupted a murder—to Gonzalo asleep it was a strange humming, to the murderers the sound of an earthquake and the roaring of lions. Solemn and strange music, then thunder and lightning, then soft music and dancing shapes accompany the magical appearance and disappearance of a banquet. The most glorious effects would have supported the enactment of the ceremony in which the images of Juno and Ceres blessed the betrothal of Ferdinand and Miranda.

I believe it is agreed that in no other play of Shakespeare's is music so vital to the conception although of course we do not have enough to help us re-create the original productions. It is, I think, a misconception—or at least, the argument is unsatisfactory—that speaks of *The Tempest* as a form developing out of masque into opera, but this I think we may say, that spectacle and music are as integral to the conception of the work as are the representation of persons and the movement of verse and meanings. And the marvels we behold together with music that would have been worthy of the songs would give the finally lasting impress to the metaphysical and religious postulates that underly the action. Mr. J. H. Long could not have worked out all that would finally sub-stantiate his judgment but I think we must generally agree with his idea of the play as a sustained musical movement ending in rhythmic and harmonic resolution.[7]

The notion of a single, completed movement led Prospero to liken the existences of humans and of the world to a pageant, but Shakespeare's perspective of the form of the play is not precisely this. Prospero had acted in bringing certain matters to a conclusion, and in laying down his task he is preparing for death. He has hopes for those who are succeeding him and for those who are yet to come, but his own perspective is that of one whose power is now gone and whose life shortly will be. It is his work and life that is vanishing. Much has been as he planned, and he has looked upon all that has happened as one apart from it. Ariel, by contrast, time and time again speaks as from within the very processes of things, as at the source of the power Prospero has solicited and depended on. The form of the play is established in relating the realm in which Ariel has his being to that of Prospero. It is accordingly not defined as a journey or a procession that is over with but as a celebration of what is and what is to come. The climax of the play is in the ceremonial in which images of goddesses bless the future.

Prospero in arranging to right wrongs and provide for Miranda and in coping with his unwilling minister and servant and those who plot against him submitted himself to an order in things he had learned something of. His magic, his solicitation of memory, and his prescience all attest to his respect for a special hierarchy of demonic powers that he had come to understand at least partly. But he was equally respectful of powers he made no claim to fathom—fortune, the ways of time, destiny, providence. He deferred to all these, indeed he honored them, and he used enough of the language of orthodox Christian doctrine to make it certain he had no interest in going beyond the prerogatives of humans. He could only solicit, not govern. He did not even claim the authority of a priest, blessing, pardoning. He was far from being the intermediary of grace. At most he prays:

> Fair encounter
> Of two most rare affections! Heavens rain grace
> On that which breeds between 'em! (III. i. 74-6)

The ways of fortune and destiny he knew were beyond his comprehension, and that he must work with them—it was through these his enemies were brought within his power, and it was through destiny and providence that this should be at a time when there could be a betrothal for his daughter. He knows himself to be subject to the laws that put spirits to the service of men as well as to something he cannot define that he yet recognizes to be at work in the ways in which time brings things to pass. His effectiveness depends upon obedience, his doing right depends on it, his freedom is in choosing to obey the right. And then he must resign his power, leave to nature and fortune and destiny the future of those he has so cared for. He had fostered the union, he had, so to speak, offered to the gods. Now he would depart, the task never to be finished by him, he returning to that death in which fish might feed upon his flesh, and his bones, too, might become coral, all that was certain would be that he would be ending in the fated ways of all things, lifeless, powerless.

In a certain obvious respect Prospero acted to obtain what King Lear dreamed of, the consolation that redeems suffering, and his conception of what the gods wanted led him to act out the vision suffering engendered. The authority of the idea of blessedness in *Lear* is in the power of the representation of human suffering and how in such as the king it is instrumental in purification and in ennoblement. But in *The Tempest* all that is in the abyss of the past, and Prospero is not among the sainted, as Lear madly imagined he might be, he is alive and sane and burdened. He cannot afford the illusion of believing he and another Cordelia might pass eternity in God's kind nursery, he must merely make the best of things.

If one wishes to call this motive love, and to agree that here as in so many of the sonnets and in *King Lear* Shakespeare is allowing it such power as the gods possess, yet one must say that the governing conception of *The Tempest* is not in the celebration of love as such, whatever its authority, but of what has brought life into being and consigned it to the care of humans. What governs the play, I think, is the conception of being that Shakespeare earlier sounded in *The Phœnix and Turtle*. For such a conception the idea of love which perhaps inevitably carries with it a personal and human character is too limiting.[8]

NOTES

[1] A. D. Nuttall, *Two Concepts of Allegory, A Study of Shakespeare's The Tempest and the Logic of Allegorical Expression*, London, 1967, p. 147.

[2] *The Elizabethan Love Sonnet*, London, 1956, p. 276.
Professor Nuttall, in the most adept philosophical treatment we so far have of *The Tempest*, has taken up the meanings that Mr. Lever has analyzed so finely and extended them: 'The concept of extended duration at last gives way to the frankly metaphysical concept of eternity when the two strands of the Sonnets—the intricate love story and the horror of mutability—are joined in the third remedy, love. It was not the poet's verses that should free his friend from the tyranny of time, but rather his love. Love itself (the now-familiar locution is forced upon us) is timeless and invulnerable.' (*Two Concepts of Allegory*, p. 122).
In *The Tempest* itself, with its insistent suggestions of the metaphysical, Mr. Nuttall continues, 'Love *is* conceived as a supernatural force, and any number of protestations of metaphor and apologetic inverted commas cannot do away with the fact that a sort of deification, and therefore *a fortiori* reification has taken place. Whether these concepts

should be allowed to be meaningful, or whether they should be permitted only a "merely aesthetic" force (and that presumably spurious) I do not know. The unassertive candour of Shakespeare's imagination has left the question open.' (p. 160).

We have long understood that it is not only in *The Tempest* we must come to terms with what Shakespeare is doing with the suggestions of supernatural power and benevolence. Sooner or later we arrive at whatever conclusions we judge proper when it is proposed that Shakespeare is depending upon Christian faith. For my part I believe that the effects of the poetry itself—this communication of the quality I have spoken of as stillness and serenity—should initially be referred to that state the ancients spoke of as close to the divine. This is a character I think we must allow such expression in Shakespeare whether or not we are drawn to other conclusions as well. On this matter we may be grateful for the summary M. Ragnar Holte provides: 'Si l'on cherche à condenser en une formule générale ce que signifie εὐδαιμονία pour un Grec, on peut dire—nous laissons ici de côté les sens affaiblis, secondaires—qu'il désigne un idéal de vie amenant les hommes aussi près de la vie des dieux qu'ils peuvent en avoir le désir sans pour autant se rendre coupables de démesure, ὕβρις. . . . L'εὐδαιμονία est l'état de l'homme òu l'élément divin n'est ni affaibli ni étouffé, mais se trouve au contraire actualisé avec son maximum de plénitude et de force, les autres puissances vitales étant soit déracinées soit soumises à sa direction. Cet état est toujours conçu comme dépendant de la vertu, ἀρετή, surtout de la plus haute des vertus, la sagesse, φοφία, ou comme s'identifiant avec elle.' (*Béatitude et Sagesse, Saint Augustin et le problème de la fin de l'homme dans la philosophie ancienne*, Paris, 1962, pp. 14-15.

[3] John Armstrong, *The Paradise Myth*, London, 1969, p. 46.

[4] *Two Concepts of Allegory*, pp. 156-7.

[5] The Aristotelean sense here agrees in important respects with the Platonic: '"To be" anything, in the world of natural processes, means "to be something that comes into being and passes away", something that is subject to change. In this sense, anything that is, any *ousia*, is anything that is what it is as the result of a process, a *kinesis*.' (J. H. Randall, *Aristotle*, New York, 1960, p. 111).

This is the argument of the *Metaphysics*, and here as well as in *On Philosophy* Werner Jaeger believes that Aristotle carries on the Platonic notion that the best (*ariston*) and the purest reality (*ousia*) coincide. (*Aristotle*, Oxford, 1948, p. 222).

In *The Tempest* Shakespeare does not of course introduce either the terms or the arguments that would point us towards certain refinements of speculation, nor does he, as Marston and Jonson on occasion do, supply footnotes in reference. Nor, however carefully articulated we judge the reasoning of *The Phœnix and Turtle* or any other work to be, may we refer to that for precise corroboration when any number of modifications would be possible from moment to moment. One is merely required to refer to what in traditional thought is coherent with conceptions developed in the particular work.

6 *The Dream of Prospero*, Oxford, 1967, p. 39.

7 *Shakespeare's Use of Music: The Final Comedies*, Gainesville, 1961, p. 96: 'Let us consider the play as some great plagal cadence whose passing chords are resolved by the soul-satisfying completeness and finality of the tonic chord.'

8 The integrity of this composition is such one is bound to relate the political and ethical matters that arise in representing the claims of liberty and subordination to the more general matters that come to mind in reflecting upon Prospero's abjuring of power and upon the temper with which the play ends. This calls for still other perspectives one is obliged to take account of in any effort at a summary.

It is of course impossible to identify the state of mind the play leads to in its conclusion with any other than the author's own resolution of the issues that arose in handling his material. But where so much has to do with obedience and with the recognition of divine powers it would be remiss to exclude from any summary estimate the consideration of a certain Christian perspective upon such matters. I have already cited words of M. Ragnar Holte in characterizing the serenity within the grasp of the ancients to help us in assessing not only Prospero's quietness at the end, but elsewhere, such as Hamlet's also, when he speaks of the felicity he credits Horatio with, and Horatio's state, also, in commending the soul of his friend to the care of angels. The traditional Christian view may offer even more light in helping us reflect upon the conclusion of *The Tempest*, particularly as we keep in mind that this is looking towards the celebration of a marriage with all that that implies. In exploring such a perspective, M. Holte's further observations can be of great help: '... les deux traits de l'amour, la joie et la subordination, ne peuvent entrer en conflit, si l'homme se conduit bien. Ils forment un tout, fondé sus la structure ontologique de la charité (conçue selon le couple *participatio-imago*). Cette unité est déjà exprimée dans la notion *Deo propter seipsum frui*, laquelle signifie un don du sujet à un objet situé en dehors de lui. Sans doute le moi ne cesse jamais d'être sujet de l'amour—

comment cela serait-il possible?—et jamais non plus l'amour ne peut oublier qu'il s'adresse à celui dont il attend tout bien—sinon il se rendrait coupable d'un péché grave d'ingratitude. . . .

'Nous comprenons maintenant comment Augustin peut identifier le désir de la béatitude avec la recherche de Dieu. Dieu est *beata vita*, il y a plaisir et joie à l'aimer: Dieu est volonté, l'aimer c'est lui obéir. Si cette unité est fondée philosophiquement sur la structure ontologique de la charité, elle a en même temps son fondement dans la théologie chrétienne de la création. L'homme est créé, pour vivre dans la béatitude, soumis à la volonté de Dieu. Augustin marque particulièrement qu'il n'est pas destiné à une béatitude exempte de soumission. Un degré aussi parfait de béatitude n'appartient qu'à celui qui possède son être et sa béatitude en soi, *per se*, à savoir Dieu lui-même. Les "notions" que possède l'homme même déchu, constituent des exhortations à realiser sa vocation, qui lui est donnée dans sa création même. Mais l'homme dans l'état déchu ne prend point plaisir à la volonté de Dieu, il est au contraire dominé par le désir d'être son propre maître (*superbia*). Alors qu'il était créé pour la béatitude sous la souveraineté de Dieu, voilà qu'il ne cherche plus que le plaisir à l'exclusion de la soumission. Mais Dieu ne lui permet pas d'y réussir. En effet même lorsqu'il se tourne vers les choses sensibles pour en jouir avec un amour qui vise à la *fruitio propter seipsam rei*, cet amour le pousse à une subordination qui va à l'encontre de ses intentions. Il devient l'esclave du sensible, il perd la maitrîse de soi-même. En prenant un être autre de Dieu pour objet de *fruitio*, il a transgressé *l'ordo*. Suivant une logique inexorable, la sanction se trouve déjà dans la structure ontologique de cet amour faux, laquelle est semblable à celle de l'amour vrai. *Frui* comporte dans les deux cas un abandon de soi et une soumission; mais, si la subordination à Dieu est liberté et béatitude, la subordination au sensible est au contraire esclavage, avilissement profond et malheur.' (*Béatitude et Sagesse*, pp. 230–1).

'L'immutabilité ne désigne pas pour Augustin un état statique, mort, mais au contraire un état de plénitude ontologique et de force, source d'une activité dynamique qui, lois d'ébranler la consistance propre de l'être, met en mouvement une existence ontologiquement inférieure. *Constantia* est une notion relative, qui n'est pas réservée à Dieu seul. L'âme aussi possede une certaine 'consistance' par comparaison avec le corps, laquelle croît si l'âme acquiert la *virtus* proprement dit, la vertu.' (pp. 233–4).

It has been observed that 'essentialism' rather than 'existentialism' provides the base for Shakespeare's conceptions, and in the Scholastic sense, being implying essence. (G. C. Herndl, *The High Design*, Lexington, 1970, pp. 50–1).

INDEX

Index